United States Government Accountability Office

Report to Congressional Requesters

I0428363

September 2013

PATRIOT EXPRESS

SBA Should Evaluate the Program and Enhance Eligibility Controls

GAO-13-727

PATRIOT EXPRESS

SBA Should Evaluate the Program and Enhance Eligibility Controls

GAO Highlights

Highlights of GAO-13-727, a report to congressional requesters

Why GAO Did This Study

In June 2007, SBA established the Patriot Express Pilot Loan Program within its 7(a) loan guarantee program to provide small businesses owned and operated by veterans and other eligible members of the military community access to capital. Through Patriot Express, SBA guarantees individual small business loans that lenders originate. GAO was asked to evaluate the program. This report examines (1) trends in the volume and performance of Patriot Express and related SBA loan programs; (2) the effect of the program on eligible members of the military community; and (3) SBA internal controls to ensure that only eligible borrowers participate. GAO analyzed data on performance and costs of Patriot Express and other similar SBA loan programs from 2007 through 2012; interviewed selected borrowers, lenders, and veteran service organizations; and reviewed SBA internal control guidance on borrower eligibility.

What GAO Recommends

SBA should design and implement an evaluation plan to assess how well the Patriot Express pilot is achieving program objectives and goals and serving the needs of veterans and eligible borrowers. Going forward, SBA should include an evaluation plan as part of any pilot programs initiated under its own authority and consider the results of the evaluation when deciding whether to extend or terminate a pilot. Further, SBA should enhance internal controls over borrower eligibility requirements. SBA said that it will consider the findings from this report as it reviewed the extension of the Patriot Express pilot.

View GAO-13-727. For more information, contact William B.Shear at (202) 512-8678 or shearw@gao.gov.

What GAO Found

Patriot Express loans valued at about $703 million have defaulted at a higher rate than loans under the Small Business Administration's (SBA) other related loan guarantee programs, and losses for Patriot Express have exceeded its income. With the exception of loans approved in 2007, Patriot Express loans have defaulted at a higher rate than loans made under SBA's main 7(a) program or loans made under SBA's streamlined loan guarantee program (SBA Express). The Patriot Express program's overall default rate was significantly higher for smaller loans, especially for loans below $25,000 (20 percent). Additionally, one lender accounted for more than 64 percent of these smaller loans and experienced higher default rates than the remaining lenders. From 2007 through 2012, losses in the Patriot Express program exceeded income by $31.1 million (not accounting for future fee revenues or funds recovered from loans in default).

Selected borrowers and lenders, as well as veteran service organizations GAO met with, reported various benefits and challenges to the Patriot Express program, but SBA has yet to evaluate the effect of this pilot program on eligible members of the military community. Borrowers and lenders said that some benefits of the program were that it helped veterans expand their businesses and allowed them to take advantage of the streamlined application process. Some challenges they identified were low awareness of the program and which lenders participated in the program. In 2010, SBA extended the Patriot Express pilot through 2013 to allow time to evaluate the effect of the program. To date, SBA has not evaluated the program or established a plan of what it intends to do to evaluate it. SBA officials told us that they focused their resources on evaluating 7(a) loans because there are many more of them and, therefore, they pose a greater risk to SBA than Patriot Express loans. In addition to Patriot Express, SBA has previously initiated other pilot programs that it has not evaluated. GAO has found that a program evaluation gives an agency the opportunity to refine program design, assess if program operations have resulted in the desired benefits, and, for pilots, determine whether to make the programs permanent. Without conducting evaluations of pilot programs, SBA lacks the information needed to assess their performance and their effects on eligible participants and decide whether to extend these programs, including Patriot Express.

SBA's internal controls over lenders may not provide reasonable assurance that Patriot Express loans are only made to eligible members of the military community and that only these members benefit from loan proceeds. SBA relies on lenders to verify and document borrower eligibility at the time of loan approval. One of SBA's controls over lenders' compliance with eligibility requirements consists of sampling loan files during examinations of the 7(a) program, but few Patriot Express loans are reviewed. Patriot Express is intended to assist only eligible members of the military community and SBA officials told us that they expect borrowers to maintain eligibility after the loan is disbursed. But SBA has not developed procedures for lenders to provide reasonable assurance that borrowers maintain this eligibility. Federal internal control standards and GAO's fraud-prevention framework indicate that ongoing monitoring is an important component of an effective internal control system. Without enhanced internal controls, particularly with respect to monitoring of borrowers, SBA lacks assurance that Patriot Express loans are serving only eligible borrowers.

_____ United States Government Accountability Office

Contents

Letter		1
	Background	4
	Patriot Express Loans Default at a Higher Rate Than Other SBA Loans, and Costs Have Exceeded Overall Program Income Since 2007	10
	Stakeholders Reported Benefits and Challenges, but SBA Has Not Evaluated the Effects of the Patriot Express Pilot	30
	SBA's Internal Controls May Not Provide Assurance of Borrower Eligibility	46
	Conclusions	51
	Recommendations for Executive Action	52
	Agency Comments	53
Appendix I	Objectives, Scope, and Methodology	55
Appendix II	Comparison of SBA's 7(a), SBA Express, and Patriot Express Loan Programs	64
Appendix III	GAO Contact and Staff Acknowledgments	67
Tables		
	Table 1: Top 11 and Remaining Lenders for Patriot Express Based on Loans Approved, 2007-2012	13
	Table 2: Average Loan Amounts, Number of Loans, and Total Dollar Amount of Loans for the Patriot Express, SBA Express, and 7(a) Programs, June 2007-2012	16
	Table 3: Patriot Express Program Fees, Recoveries, Purchases, and Net Cash Flows, Fiscal Years 2007-2012	27
	Table 4: Patriot Express Loans Sampled in Most Recent SBA Examination and Number of Patriot Express Loans Made by Top 10 Lenders from 2007 to the Year Prior to Examination	48
	Table 5: Selected Characteristics of Loan Recipients Included in Our Sample	59
	Table 6: Comparison of 7(a), SBA Express, and Patriot Express Loan Programs	64

Figures

Figure 1: Patriot Express Loan Origination Process and Costs   7

Figure 2: Purchase Process for Patriot Express Loan   9

Figure 3: Number, Average Value, and Total Value of Patriot Express Loans Approved, 2007-2012   12

Figure 4: Number, Average Value, and Total Value of SBA Express Loans Approved, 2007-2012   14

Figure 5: Number, Average Value, and Total Value of 7(a) Loans Approved, 2007-2012   15

Figure 6: Default Rates for Patriot Express, SBA Express, and 7(a) by Loan Approval Year, as of December 31, 2012   17

Figure 7: Default Rates and Number of Loans Approved for Different Loan Amounts for the Patriot Express Program, 2007-2012   18

Figure 8: Total Number of Patriot Express Loans and Default Rates by Lender and Loan Approval Year 2007-2012, as of December 31, 2012   19

Figure 9: Default Rates by Loan Amounts Approved for Patriot Express, SBA Express, and 7(a), 2007-2012   20

Figure 10: Number of Patriot Express, SBA Express, and 7(a) Loans Made to Veterans, 2001-2012   22

Figure 11: Dollar Amounts Approved for Patriot Express, SBA Express, and 7(a) Loans Made to Veterans, 2007-2012   24

Figure 12: Default Rates of Loans Made to Veterans through Patriot Express, SBA Express, and 7(a) by Year of Approval, as of December 31, 2012   25

Figure 13: Patriot Express Purchases and Offsets, Fiscal Years 2007-2012   28

Figure 14: Examples of Loan Terms for a Patriot Express, Express, 7(a), and Small Loan Advantage Loan to a Veteran Borrower   38

Abbreviations

ARRA	American Recovery and Reinvestment Act of 2009
EBV	Entrepreneurship Bootcamp for Veterans with Disabilities
FICO	Fair Isaac Corporation
GPRA	Government Performance and Results Act of 1993
GPRAMA	GPRA Modernization Act of 2010
NAGGL	National Association of Government Guaranteed Lenders
OEG	Operation Endure and Grow
OIG	Office of Inspector General
OMB	Office of Management and Budget
OVBD	Office of Veterans Business Development
PLP	Preferred Lenders Program
SBA	Small Business Administration
SBDC	Small Business Development Centers
SBLC	small business lending company
SBPS	Small Business Portfolio Solutions
SLA	Small Loan Advantage
VBOC	Veteran Business Outreach Centers
VET	Veteran Entrepreneurship Task Force
V-WISE	Veteran Women Igniting the Spirit of Entrepreneurship
WBC	Women's Business Centers

GAO U.S. GOVERNMENT ACCOUNTABILITY OFFICE

441 G St. N.W.
Washington, DC 20548

September 12, 2013

The Honorable Mary L. Landrieu
Chair
Committee on Small Business and Entrepreneurship
United States Senate

The Honorable Mark Pryor
United States Senate

Since the Small Business Administration (SBA) established the Patriot Express Pilot Loan Initiative to provide veterans and other eligible members of the military community access to capital to establish or expand small businesses in June 2007, lenders have made about $703 million in Patriot Express loans. The Patriot Express program, a pilot loan initiative under SBA's 7(a) loan guarantee program, allows lenders to use their own underwriting criteria and loan documents to expedite loan decisions for eligible borrowers.[1] Patriot Express borrowers must have a business that is owned and controlled (51 percent or more) by veterans or other eligible members of the military community.[2] The Patriot Express program provides the same loan guarantee to SBA-approved lenders as the 7(a) program and is available on loan amounts up to $500,000, and the loan proceeds can be used for the same purposes as the 7(a) loan proceeds.[3] SBA announced on December 14, 2010, that it would continue to operate the Patriot Express program through December 31, 2013.

You asked us to evaluate the program. This report examines (1) trends in the Patriot Express program and related SBA guarantee programs,

---

[1] Section 7(a) of the Small Business Act, as amended, codified at 15 U.S.C. § 636(a).

[2] Other eligible members of the military include service-disabled veterans, active duty military participating in the military's Transition Assistance Program, reservists or National Guard members or a current spouse of any of these groups, a widowed spouse of a service member who died while in service, or a widowed spouse of a veteran who died of a service-connected disability.

[3] The proceeds of 7(a) loans may be used for working capital and other general business purposes. The program is intended to serve small business borrowers who could not otherwise obtain credit under reasonable terms and conditions from the private sector without an SBA guarantee. The 7(a) program provides an 85 percent guarantee on loan amounts of $150,000 or less and a 75 percent guarantee on loan amounts over $150,000.

including performance of these loans, and what is known about the costs of the Patriot Express program, (2) the benefits and challenges of the Patriot Express program for members of the military community eligible to participate as well as training and counseling opportunities available to them, and (3) what internal controls SBA has in place to ensure that the Patriot Express program is available only to eligible members of the military community.

To describe how Patriot Express loans approved from 2007 through 2012 have performed, we obtained SBA loan-level data from the second quarter of 2007 through the fourth quarter of 2012 for the Patriot Express program and analyzed them for various performance measures, including default rates.[4] To compare the performance of Patriot Express loans to those of SBA's 7(a) and SBA Express programs, we obtained and analyzed SBA loan-level data for loans approved in these programs from 2007 through 2012 and compared default rates to those of the Patriot Express program.[5] To describe what is known about the costs of the Patriot Express program from 2007 through 2012, we obtained and analyzed SBA cash-flow data on SBA purchases of defaulted loans, as well as data on fees generated by the program and recovery rates of defaulted loans. To assess data reliability, we interviewed SBA representatives about how they collected data and helped ensure data integrity, and we reviewed internal agency procedures for ensuring data reliability. In addition, we conducted reasonableness checks on the data to identify any missing, erroneous, or outlying figures. We determined that the data were sufficiently reliable for our purposes.

To assess the effect of the Patriot Express program on members of the military community eligible to participate in the program, we selected and interviewed a nongeneralizable, stratified random sample of 24 Patriot Express loan recipients. We conducted interviews with these recipients to inquire how the Patriot Express loan affected their businesses and to

---

[4]In this report, we define the default rate as the number of loans that SBA has purchased from the lender divided by the outstanding number of loans approved.

[5]The SBA Express program is a subprogram of the 7(a) loan program and was established as a pilot program by SBA on February 27, 1995. The program was made permanent through legislation in 2004. The program was designed to increase the availability of credit to small businesses by permitting lenders to use their existing documents and procedures in return for receiving a reduced SBA guarantee on loans. It provides a 50 percent loan guarantee on loan amounts up to $350,000.

obtain their views on how the program could be improved. To obtain the perspectives of veteran entrepreneurs who were aware of the Patriot Express program and appeared to meet the eligibility requirements for a Patriot Express loan but instead obtained a 7(a) loan, we selected and interviewed a nongeneralizable stratified random sample of four veteran entrepreneurs who obtained a 7(a) loan. We conducted interviews with these recipients to inquire about their experiences with the 7(a) loan and obtain their views on the Patriot Express program. We also interviewed SBA officials and selected lenders and veteran service organizations. To describe other ways in which veteran entrepreneurs accessed capital, as part of our interviews of Patriot Express and 7(a) loan recipients, we inquired about other ways in which they had gained access to capital. For this purpose, we also interviewed selected lenders and veteran service organizations. To describe the training and counseling efforts SBA has in place for veteran entrepreneurs, we obtained and reviewed SBA annual reports and other documents related to training and counseling efforts. We also interviewed SBA officials responsible for these efforts. To obtain the perspectives of veteran entrepreneurs on the effectiveness of SBA's training and counseling efforts, we interviewed veteran service organizations and selected Patriot Express and 7(a) loan recipients.

To evaluate SBA's internal controls related to ensuring that the Patriot Express program is available only to members of the military community eligible to participate in the program, we reviewed SBA's standard operating procedures related to oversight of lenders, federal internal control standards, and GAO's fraud-prevention framework. We interviewed officials from the Office of Credit Risk Management to inquire about SBA's oversight of its lenders, including how it addresses the program's vulnerability to fraud and abuse. To determine how SBA examiners review lenders for compliance with eligibility requirements for the Patriot Express program, we reviewed examination reports for the top 10 Patriot Express lenders (based on the number of loans made) from 2007 through 2012. Finally, to help assess the extent to which the Patriot Express program could be susceptible to fraud and abuse, we reviewed SBA's internal control standards related to ensuring that Patriot Express loans were made to eligible members of the military community. We also interviewed officials from SBA's Office of Credit Risk Management and Office of Inspector General to learn about scenarios under which the Patriot Express program could be susceptible to fraud and abuse.

We conducted this performance audit from November 2012 to September 2013 in accordance with generally accepted government auditing standards. Those standards require that we plan and perform the audit to obtain sufficient, appropriate evidence to provide a reasonable basis for our findings and conclusions based on our audit objectives. We believe that the evidence obtained provides a reasonable basis for our findings and conclusions based on our audit objectives. Appendix I contains additional information on our scope and methodology.

Background

SBA was created in 1953 to assist and protect the interests of small businesses, in part by addressing constraints in the supply of credit for these firms. The 7(a) program, named after the section of the Small Business Act that authorized it, is SBA's largest business loan program.[6] The program is intended to serve creditworthy small business borrowers who cannot obtain credit through a conventional lender at reasonable terms and do not have the personal resources to provide financing themselves. Under the 7(a) program, SBA guarantees loans made by commercial lenders to small businesses for working capital and other general business purposes.[7] These lenders are mostly banks, but some are nondepository lenders, including small business lending companies (SBLC).[8] The guarantee assures the lender that if a borrower defaults on a loan, SBA will purchase the loan and the lender will receive an agreed-upon portion (generally between 50 percent and 85 percent) of the outstanding balance. For a majority of 7(a) loans, SBA relies on lenders with delegated authority to process and service 7(a) loans and to ensure that borrowers meet the program's eligibility requirements. To be eligible for the 7(a) program, a business must be an operating for-profit small firm (according to SBA's size standards) located in the United States and

---

[6]Section 7(a) of the Small Business Act, as amended, and now codified at 15 U.S.C. Section 636(a), provides the authority for the 7(a) program.

[7]SBA has limited legislative authority to make direct loans to borrowers unable to obtain loans from conventional lenders.

[8]In addition to depository institutions, SBA has authorized other types of lenders to make SBA-guaranteed loans. These lenders include SBLCs, which are generally not subject to oversight and examination by a federal financial institution regulator. SBLCs are nondepository lenders that enter into agreements with SBA to provide 7(a) loans and microloans to qualified small businesses. By statute, SBA is the primary federal regulator for SBLCs and conducts safety and soundness examinations of these institutions.

meet the "credit elsewhere" requirement, including the personal resources test.[9]

Within the 7(a) program, there are several delivery methods—including regular 7(a), the Preferred Lenders Program (PLP), and SBA Express. Under the regular (nondelegated) 7(a) programs, SBA makes the loan approval decision, including the credit determination. Under PLP and SBA Express, SBA delegates to the lender the authority to make loan approval decisions, including credit determinations, without prior review by SBA. The maximum loan amount under the SBA Express program is $350,000 (as opposed to $5 million for 7(a) loans). This program allows lenders to utilize, to the maximum extent possible, their respective loan analyses, procedures, and documentation. In return for the expanded authority and autonomy provided by the program, SBA Express lenders agree to accept a maximum SBA guarantee of 50 percent. Regular (nondelegated) 7(a) loans and delegated 7(a) loans made by PLP lenders generally have a maximum guarantee of 75 or 85 percent, depending on the loan amount.[10]

In June 2007, under its own authority, SBA established the Patriot Express pilot loan program, which has features that are similar to those of the SBA Express and other 7(a) loan programs. Like the SBA Express program, the Patriot Express program allows lenders to use their own loan analyses and documents to expedite loan decisions for eligible

---

[9]In establishing size standards, SBA considers economic characteristics of the industry, including degree of competition, average firm size, start-up costs and entry barriers, and distribution of firms by size. It also considers growth trends, competition from other industries, and unique factors within an industry that may distinguish small firms from other firms. SBA's size standards seek to ensure that a firm that meets a specific size standard is not dominant in its field of operation. In addition, the Small Business Act specifies that SBA shall not make or guarantee loans for borrowers who are able to obtain credit elsewhere, which is defined as "the availability of credit from non-Federal sources on reasonable terms and conditions taking into consideration the prevailing rates and terms in the community in or near where the concern transacts business, or the homeowner resides, for similar purposes and periods of time." See, 15 U.S.C. § 636(a)(1); 15 U.S.C. § 632(h). Further, SBA requires lenders to ensure that the borrower or any principal of the business do not have the personal resources to cover the needed funding.

[10]The 7(a) program formally includes all subprograms, including Patriot Express and SBA Express. However, in this report, when we make comparisons of loan volume, performance, and benefits and challenges of Patriot Express to SBA Express and 7(a), we use "7(a) loans" to refer to both (1) regular (nondelegated) 7(a) loans and (2) delegated 7(a) loans made by PLP lenders but excluding Patriot Express and SBA Express, unless otherwise noted.

borrowers. However, the Patriot Express has a different guarantee rate than SBA Express and different eligibility requirements. Patriot Express borrowers must have a business that is owned and controlled (51 percent or more) by the following members of the military community:

- veterans (other than dishonorably discharged),

- service-disabled veterans,

- active duty military participating in the military's Transition Assistance Program,

- reservists or National Guard members,

- spouse of any of these groups,

- a widowed spouse of a service member who died while in service, or

- a widowed spouse of a veteran who died of a service-connected disability.

Like the 7(a) program, the Patriot Express program provides the same loan guarantee to SBA-approved lenders on loan amounts up to $500,000, and the loan proceeds can be used for the same purposes. SBA initially intended to operate the Patriot Express pilot for about 3 years, after which it would evaluate the program. However, SBA announced on December 14, 2010, that it would continue to operate the program for at least 3 more years to allow the agency to evaluate the program. SBA determined that it was premature to assess the results of the pilot because most of the loans were made in the previous 2 years and there had not been enough time to measure their performance. Appendix II compares the key features of the Patriot Express program to those of the regular 7(a) and SBA Express programs. Figure 1 depicts the Patriot Express loan process, including the roles played by the lender and SBA in the transaction and the fees associated with the loans.

Figure 1: Patriot Express Loan Origination Process and Costs

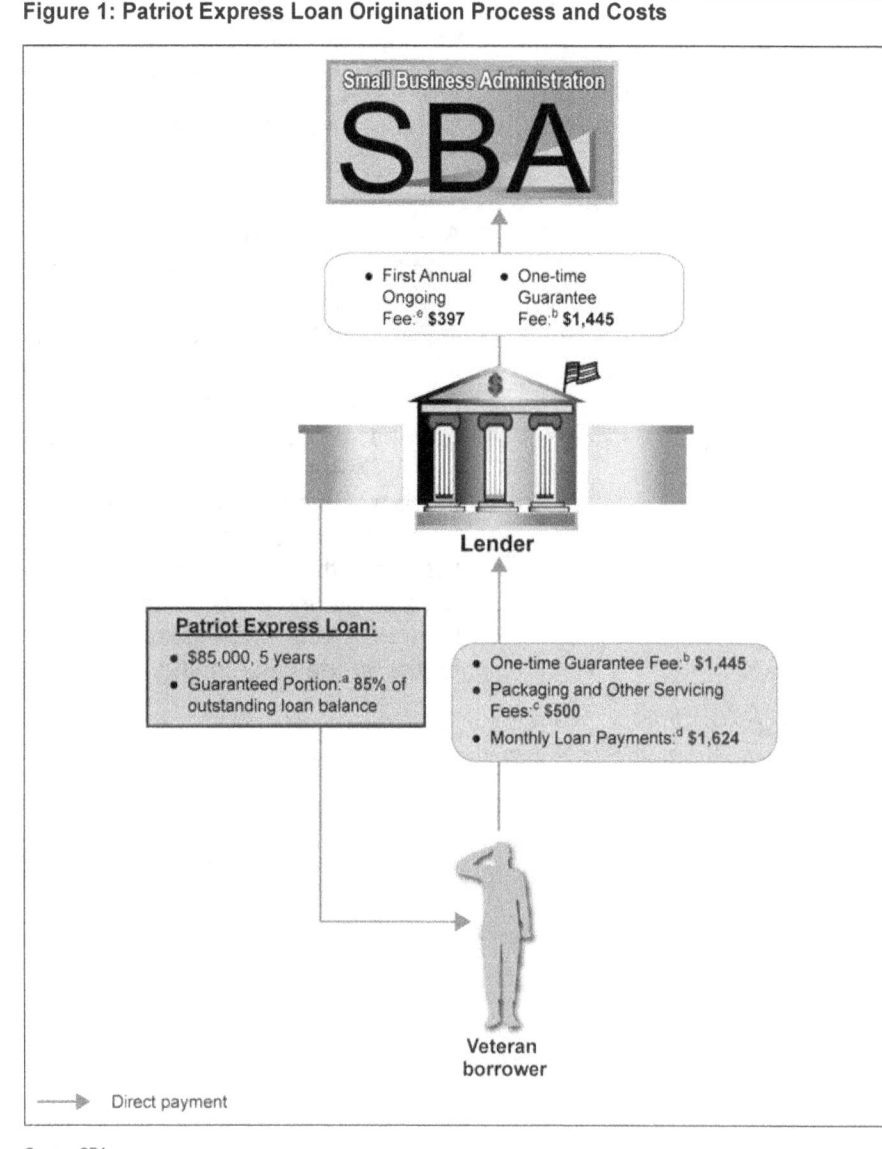

Source: SBA.

[a]The guaranteed portion is the percentage of the loan balance that SBA agrees to cover if the borrower defaults on the loan.

[b]The lender is required to pay SBA a one-time guarantee fee that is a percentage of the guaranteed portion. This fee can be passed on to the borrower and is paid within 90 days of loan approval. For this example, the guarantee fee was 2 percent of the guaranteed amount and was passed on to the borrower.

[c]"Packaging services" include assisting the applicant with completing the application, such as preparing a business plan and cash-flow projections. "Other services" include consulting fees related to the need for financing and the type of financing, as well as broker fees or referral fees. These fees

are optional and SBA guidelines state that the fees must be reasonable and customary for the services actually performed and must be consistent with those charged on the lender's similarly-sized, non-SBA-guaranteed loans.

[d]For this example, the payment was calculated by assuming the prime interest rate was 3.25 percent for an $85,000 Patriot Express loan with a term of 60 months (5 years).

[e]The lender is required to pay SBA an annual ongoing fee, and the amount is not to exceed 0.55 percent. Because the fee is applied to the outstanding balance of the guaranteed portion of the loan, the amount of this fee will change every year. This fee cannot be passed onto the borrower.

A lender may request that SBA honor its guarantee by purchasing the loan if a borrower is in default on an SBA loan for more than 60 calendar days and if the borrower is unable to cure the loan after working with the lender. The lender is required by regulation to liquidate all business personal property collateral before demanding that SBA honor the guarantee.[11] As shown in figure 2, after the lender has liquidated all business personal property collateral, it submits the purchase request to one of SBA's Office of Financial Program Operation's centers, which processes loan guarantee requests. The center reviews the lender's package to determine if it has complied with SBA rules and regulations. If SBA finds that the lender has complied with the agency's rules and regulations and conducted proper due diligence when originating the loan, SBA honors the guarantee and pays the lender the guaranteed portion of the outstanding loan amount.

---

[11]SBA's collateral policies for Patriot Express loans vary depending on the loan amount. For example, no collateral is required for Patriot Express loans of less than $25,000. However, lenders that make Patriot Express loans above $350,000 are required to collateralize the loan to the maximum extent possible up to the loan amount. If business assets do not fully secure the loan, the lender must take available personal assets of the principals as collateral. SBA considers liquidation of business personal property collateral to be completed when a lender has exhausted all prudent and commercially reasonable efforts to collect upon these assets.

Figure 2: Purchase Process for Patriot Express Loan

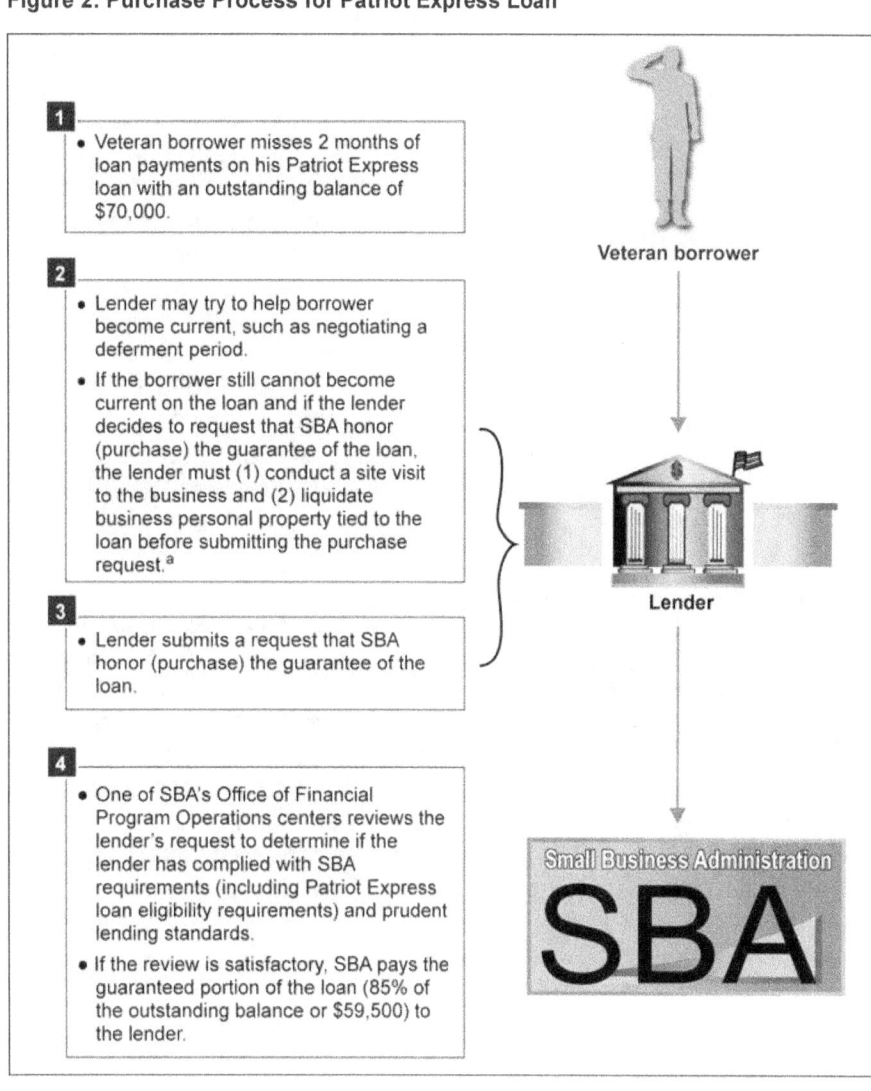

Source: SBA.

[a]According to SBA, for loans approved on or after May 14, 2007, a lender may demand in writing that SBA honor its guarantee if the borrower is in default on any installment for more than 60 calendar days and the default has not been cured, provided all business personal property securing the defaulted SBA loan has been liquidated.

According to SBA officials, the 7(a) program—including its subprograms, such as SBA Express and Patriot Express—is projected to be a "zero subsidy" program in fiscal year 2014, meaning that the program does not require annual appropriations of budget authority for new loan guarantees.[12] To offset some of the costs of the program, such as the costs of purchasing defaulted loans, SBA assesses lenders two fees on each 7(a) loan, including Patriot Express loans. The guarantee fee must be paid by the lender at the time of application for the guarantee or within 90 days of the loan being approved, depending upon the loan term. This fee is based on the amount of the loan and the level of the guarantee, and lenders can pass the fee on to the borrower. The ongoing servicing fee must be paid annually by the lender and is based on the outstanding balance of the guaranteed portion of the loan.

SBA's Office of Credit Risk Management is responsible for overseeing 7(a) lenders, including those with delegated authority. SBA created this office in fiscal year 1999 to better ensure consistent and appropriate supervision of SBA's lending partners.[13] The office is responsible for managing all activities regarding lender oversight, including lender risk ratings and lender activities, and preparing written reports based on such oversight.

Patriot Express Loans Default at a Higher Rate Than Other SBA Loans, and Costs Have Exceeded Overall Program Income Since 2007

From 2007 through 2012, SBA made 8,511 Patriot Express loans. The majority of these loans were valued below $150,000, and close to half were uncollateralized loans valued below $25,000. Although Patriot Express loans represent a fraction of SBA's larger loan portfolio and are concentrated among 11 lenders, these loans have defaulted at higher rates compared to similar SBA loans made in the same time frame. At the current default and recovery rates, the costs of the Patriot Express program will likely continue to exceed overall program income.

---

[12]Credit subsidy costs represent the net present value of expected lifetime cash flows, excluding administrative costs. The subsidy rate reflects the net present value cost for each dollar of credit assistance. According to SBA, the Patriot Express program does not have a separate subsidy rate. The 7(a) subsidy rate is also applied to the Patriot Express program.

[13]Prior to reorganization in May 2007, the office was called the Office of Lender Oversight.

Lenders Have Made 8,511 Patriot Express Loans Since 2007

From the start of the program through the fourth quarter of 2012, lenders made a total of 8,511 Patriot Express loans. Taken together, these loans are valued at $702,753,406, with an average of about $82,570 per loan. As shown in figure 3, after a rapid expansion in the first 2 years of the program from 2007 through 2009, the number of Patriot Express loans declined from 2,176 approved in 2009 to 869 approved in 2012. Similarly, the total loan amounts of Patriot Express loans approved each year grew from approximately $67 million in 2007 to over $150 million in 2008 and 2009, but have since decreased. The higher numbers of Patriot Express loans approved in 2009 and 2010 may be attributable, in part, to the American Recovery and Reinvestment Act of 2009 (ARRA)[14] and subsequent legislation, which provided funding to temporarily subsidize the overall 7(a) guarantee program's fees and to increase the maximum loan guarantee percentage from 75 or 85 percent to 90 percent, with the exception of loans approved under the SBA Express 7(a) subprogram.[15] With a 5 to 15 percent increase in the maximum allowed guarantee through ARRA, lenders had a greater incentive to approve SBA loans in general (including Patriot Express loans), knowing that SBA would guarantee a higher percentage of the loan. Figure 3 also shows that average loan amounts have varied over the years. For loans approved in 2007, the average loan amount was for about $100,000, decreasing to about $70,000 in 2009, and increasing since then to just under $100,000 in 2012.

[14]The American Recovery and Reinvestment Act of 2009 (ARRA). Pub. L. No. 111-5 Division A. Title V. §§ 501, 502, 123 Stat. 115, 151-153 (2009), enacted on February 17, 2009, permitted the temporary reduction of fees in the 7(a), Patriot Express, and 504/CDC loan guarantee programs until September 30, 2010, or until $375 million of appropriated funds was expended and increased the 7(a) program's maximum loan guarantee percentage to 90 percent for all standard 7(a) loans except for SBA Express loans.

[15]For example, the Small Business Jobs Act of 2010, Pub. L. No. 111-240. §§ 1111,1114, 124 Stat. 2504, 2507, 2508 (2010) provided funding to extend the fee subsidies and 90 percent loan guarantee percentage through December 31, 2010 or until available funds were exhausted. Also, the Continuing Appropriations and Surface Transportation Extensions Act, 2011, Pub. L. No. 111-322. § 1(a)(2), 124 Stat. 3518, 3520 (2011), authorized SBA to continue the fee subsidies and the 7(a) program's 90 percent maximum loan guarantee through March 4, 2011.

Figure 3: Number, Average Value, and Total Value of Patriot Express Loans Approved, 2007-2012

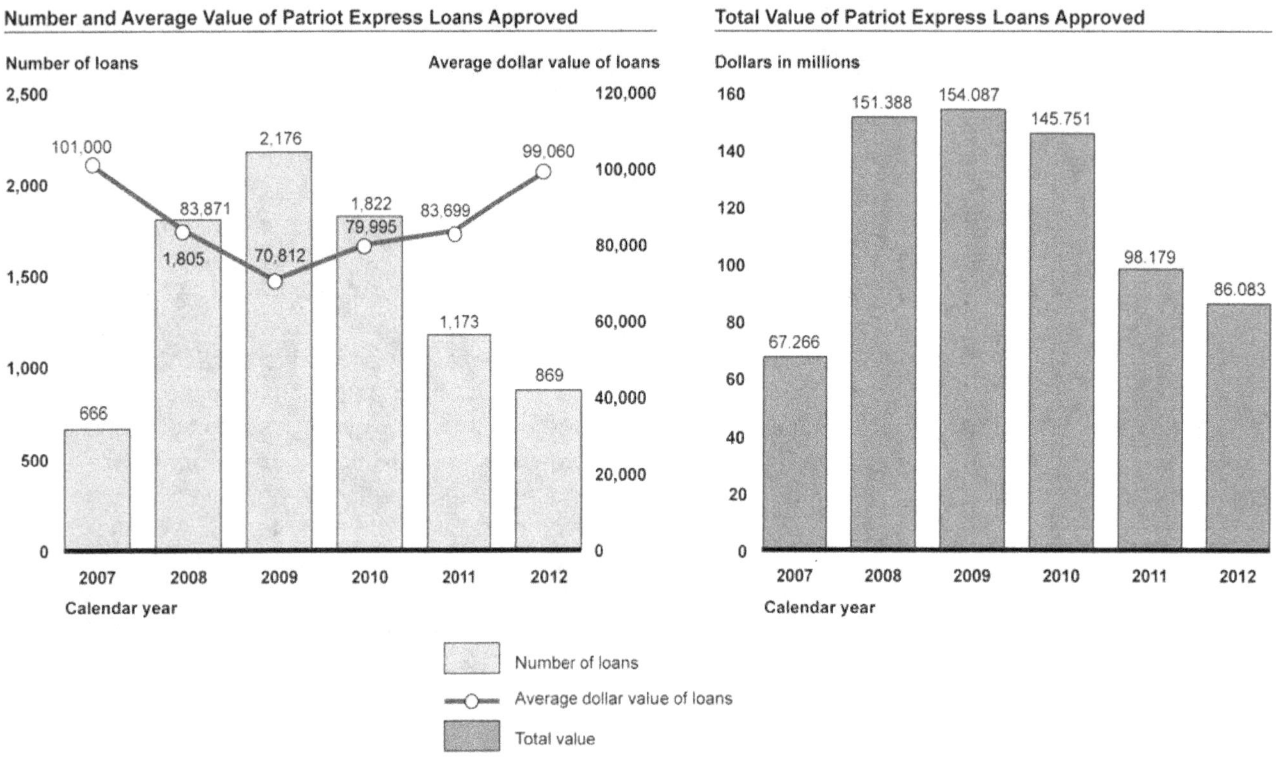

Number and Average Value of Patriot Express Loans Approved

Total Value of Patriot Express Loans Approved

Source: GAO analysis of SBA data.

Based on our analysis of SBA data from 2007 through 2012, about 67 percent of borrowers used Patriot Express loans for working capital, and about half of these loans funded businesses that were either new or had been in existence for less than 2 years. The majority of Patriot Express loans approved since the program's inception are valued at 30 percent of the maximum loan limit, and about half are small enough that they do not require collateral. Although SBA allows Patriot Express loans of up to $500,000, about 84.2 percent of the loans made since 2007 (7,166) were below $150,000. Further, 41.2 percent of Patriot Express loans (3,509) were $25,000 or less. More than 64 percent of loans up to $25,000 were provided by one lender and this lender accounted for about 26 percent of total loans in the program. This lender primarily provided loans between $5,000 and $25,000, and its average Patriot Express loan made from 2008 through 2012 was $9,759. As noted previously, loans under the Patriot Express program below $25,000 do not require collateral.

The Patriot Express program is highly concentrated in a small number of lenders. For example, the top 11 lenders (in terms of number of loans made) represent 52 percent of the Patriot Express loans made since the program's inception (see table 1). These top 11 lenders accounted for 27.55 percent of the total amount approved for the Patriot Express program. This concentration is explained, in part, by one lender that focuses on providing low-dollar loans to veteran-owned businesses and represents about 26 percent of the Patriot Express program, as discussed previously. In contrast, the remaining 782 lenders that participate in Patriot Express have approved fewer loans. For example, 246 of these 782 lenders approved one loan each since the program began in 2007.

Table 1: Top 11 and Remaining Lenders for Patriot Express Based on Loans Approved, 2007-2012

	Average loan amount	Number of loans	Percentage of total number of loans approved	Total amount approved	Percentage of total amount approved
Lender 1	$9,759	2,248	26.41%	$21,937,500	3.12%
Next 10 lenders	79,154	2,169	25.48	171,684,100	24.43
Remaining lenders (782)	124,360	4,094	48.10	509,131,806	72.45
Total		8,511		$702,753,406	

Source: GAO analysis of SBA data.

Note: Total percentage may not equal 100% due to rounding.

The Patriot Express Program Is Much Smaller Than the SBA Express or 7(a) Programs

As previously discussed, in addition to reviewing data on the Patriot Express program from 2007 through 2012, we also reviewed similar data from two other SBA loan programs: the SBA Express program and SBA's 7(a) program. SBA Express and the 7(a) program, which are not limited to borrowers in the military community, are significantly larger than the Patriot Express program. Since 2007, the SBA Express program has surpassed Patriot Express in total number of loans (156,280) and total amount ($10.9 billion) approved, but the average loan amounts for Patriot Express are larger than those for SBA Express. SBA Express has seen a decline in loan numbers and amounts approved since 2007 (see fig. 4). The number of SBA Express loans approved each year declined by about 50 percent from 2007 through 2008, and that number has remained at lower levels since then. SBA officials told us that part of the decline from 2007 through 2008 may have been due to the economic downturn, which prompted lenders to cut back on these loans. Figure 4 also shows the total value of SBA Express loans peaked in 2007 ($2.9 billion) but then decreased by nearly half in 2008 ($1.7 billion). The total value of SBA

Express loans then increased to about $2 billion in 2011 before falling to about $1.3 billion in 2012.

Figure 4: Number, Average Value, and Total Value of SBA Express Loans Approved, 2007-2012

Number and Average Value of SBA Express Loans Approved

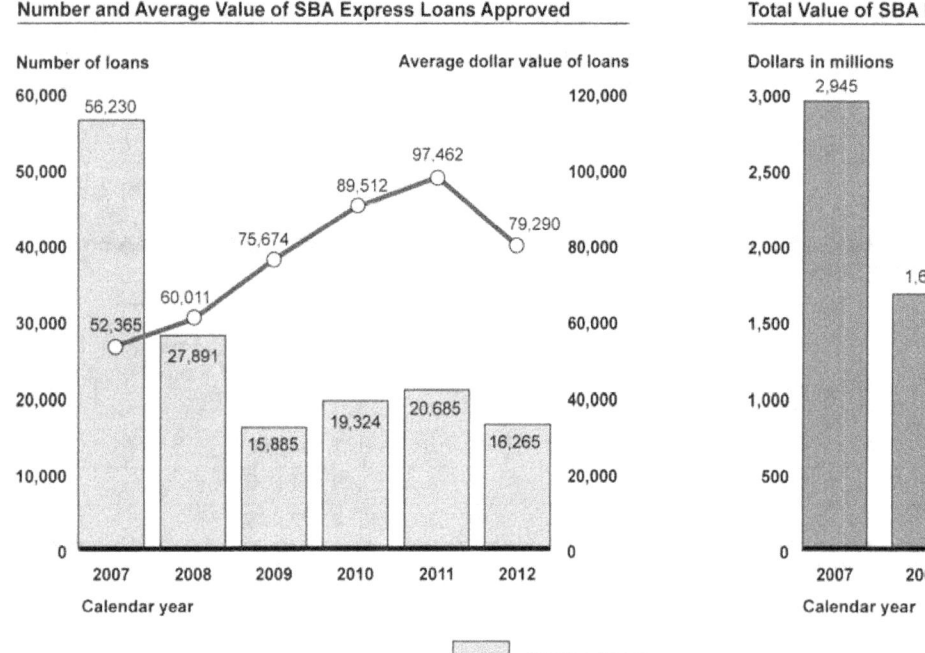

Total Value of SBA Express Loans Approved

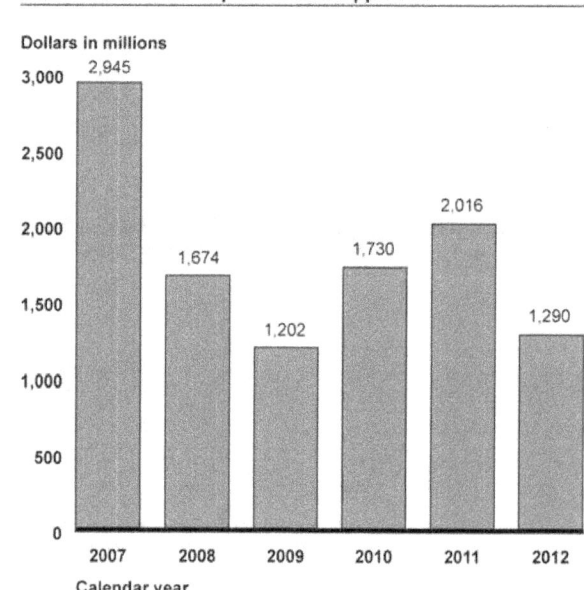

Source: GAO analysis of SBA data.

The 7(a) program is also significantly larger than the Patriot Express program in all measures, including total numbers of loans approved, average loan amounts, and total loan amounts approved. Annually, the total numbers of 7(a) loans approved have declined since peaking in 2010 at 19,131, while the average loan amount for 7(a) approvals annually has steadily increased from about $470,784 in 2007 to $716,489 in 2012 (see fig. 5). The total value of 7(a) loans approved within each year has been relatively steady, as shown in figure 5, ranging from around $7.7 billion to around $9.2 billion, with the exception of 2010, when the total value of loans approved was around $12 billion.

Figure 5: Number, Average Value, and Total Value of 7(a) Loans Approved, 2007-2012

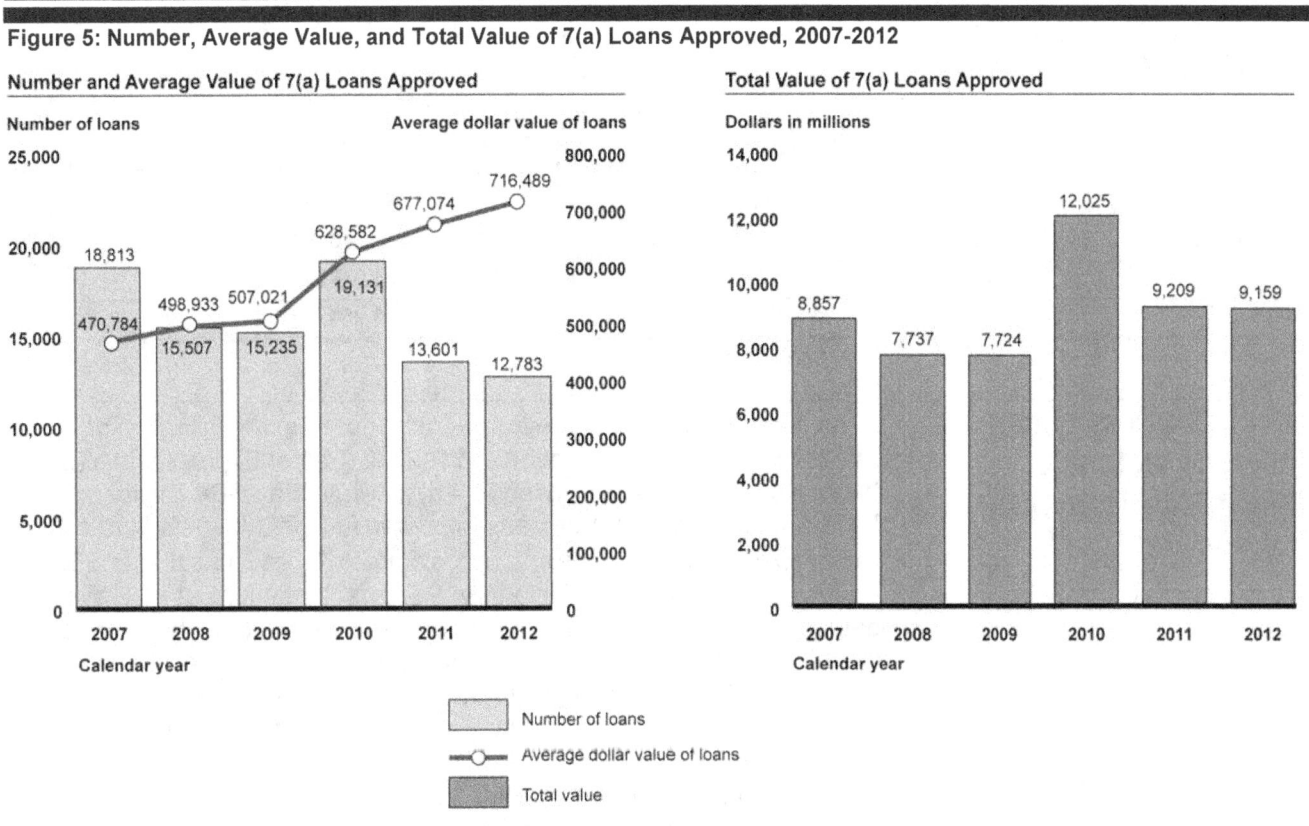

Source: GAO analysis of SBA data.

Table 2 shows the total numbers of loans, total dollar values, and average loan amounts approved for Patriot Express, SBA Express, and 7(a) from June 2007 through 2012. Additionally, the table shows the relative percentage of loans made and dollar values for each program when compared among all three programs. When comparing the three programs since the inception of Patriot Express in June 2007 through the end of 2012, Patriot Express is significantly smaller than SBA Express and 7(a) in terms of number of total loans approved (3.76 percent) and dollar amount (1.15 percent). However, the average loan amount for Patriot Express is larger than the average loan approved under SBA Express.

Table 2: Average Loan Amounts, Number of Loans, and Total Dollar Amount of Loans for the Patriot Express, SBA Express, and 7(a) Programs, June 2007-2012

	Average loan amount	Number of loans	Percentage of total number of loans approved	Total dollar amount	Percentage of total amount approved
Patriot Express	$82,570	8,511	3.76%	$702,753,406	1.15%
SBA Express	73,194	130,385	57.67	9,543,343,424	15.57
7(a)	585,431	87,192	38.57	51,044,912,552	83.28
Total		226,088		$61,291,009,382	

Source: GAO analysis of SBA data.

Patriot Express Loans Generally Default at a Higher Rate Than SBA Express and 7(a) Loans

When comparing loans approved in each year from the inception of Patriot Express through December 31, 2012, Patriot Express loans (with the exception of 2007) defaulted at a higher rate than SBA Express or 7(a) loans (see fig. 6).[16] For loans approved in 2009, the default rate for Patriot Express was 17 percent, approximately three times that of SBA Express and 7(a) loans. Additionally, the default rate for Patriot Express loans approved in 2010 was 7.4 percent, again more than three times that of SBA Express and 7(a) loans. Loans approved in more recent years have had a shorter amount of time during which to observe defaults, which may at least partially explain lower default rates in more recent years of the program.[17] The higher default rates for Patriot Express are generally consistent with one of the key measures of creditworthiness that SBA collects, the Small Business Portfolio Solutions (SBPS) scores.[18] For

---

[16]We calculated defaults by examining the number of loans that were purchased by SBA (as of December 31, 2012) based on the year that the loan was approved. As mentioned earlier, lenders can request that SBA purchase a loan if a borrower is in default on an SBA loan for more than 60 calendar days and if a borrower is unable to cure the loan after working with the lender. A loan is in default when a borrower fails to make a regular installment of principal and/or interest when due to the lender.

[17]The average time to default, as measured by the time period from approval to purchase of the defaulted loan by SBA, was 34 months for 7(a) and SBA Express, and 28 months for Patriot Express.

[18]SBPS is a credit score specific to small business that each SBA loan receives on a quarterly basis. It is an off-the-shelf product produced by the Fair Isaac Corporation (FICO) and Dun & Bradstreet. It uses Dun & Bradstreet's commercial and TransUnion's consumer credit bureau data for all disbursed and outstanding 7(a) loans. It includes business data reported by third parties, such as venders, utilities, and insurance companies. SBPS is categorized by risk (high, medium, and low) and contains a range of credit scores consistent with each level of risk.

example, 61.6 percent and 52.1 percent of 7(a) and SBA Express loans approved from 2007 through 2012 had SBPS scores of 180 or greater, compared to just 48.3 percent of Patriot Express loans approved in the same time period. Finally, although the economic downturn may account for some of the overall higher default rates in all three programs from 2007 through 2009, Patriot Express has maintained a higher default rate compared to SBA Express and 7(a) since 2008.

Figure 6: Default Rates for Patriot Express, SBA Express, and 7(a) by Loan Approval Year, as of December 31, 2012

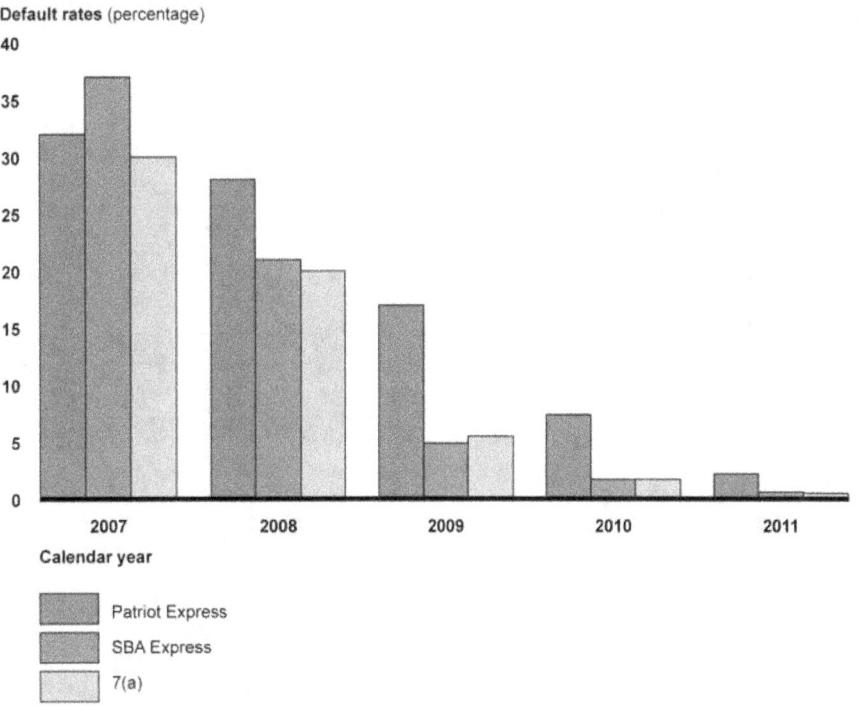

Source: GAO analysis of SBA data.

Note: This figure presents default rates for Patriot Express, SBA Express, and 7(a) as of December 31, 2012. We did not include the default rate for loans approved in 2012 because too little time had passed as of December 31, 2012, to fully assess the default rate for this cohort. The Patriot Express program began on June 28, 2007. In the figure, we present 2007 default rates for the entire year for the 7(a) and SBA Express programs. Limiting our analysis to July 1, 2007, for Patriot Express, SBA Express, and 7(a) produced similar results. Starting in 2008, one lender that specialized in Patriot Express loans valued up to $25,000 began approving loans that defaulted at a higher rate than loans approved by other lenders. A more detailed comparison of this lender to other Patriot Express lenders is shown later in figure 8.

The default rates for the Patriot Express program are generally higher for the smaller loan amounts. For example, as shown in figure 7, loans under $10,000, which represent 21.3 percent of all Patriot Express loans from

2007 through 2012, had an overall 22 percent default rate. Additionally, Patriot Express loans under $25,000, which represent 41.2 percent of loans made in the same period, had a default rate of 20 percent.

Figure 7: Default Rates and Number of Loans Approved for Different Loan Amounts for the Patriot Express Program, 2007-2012

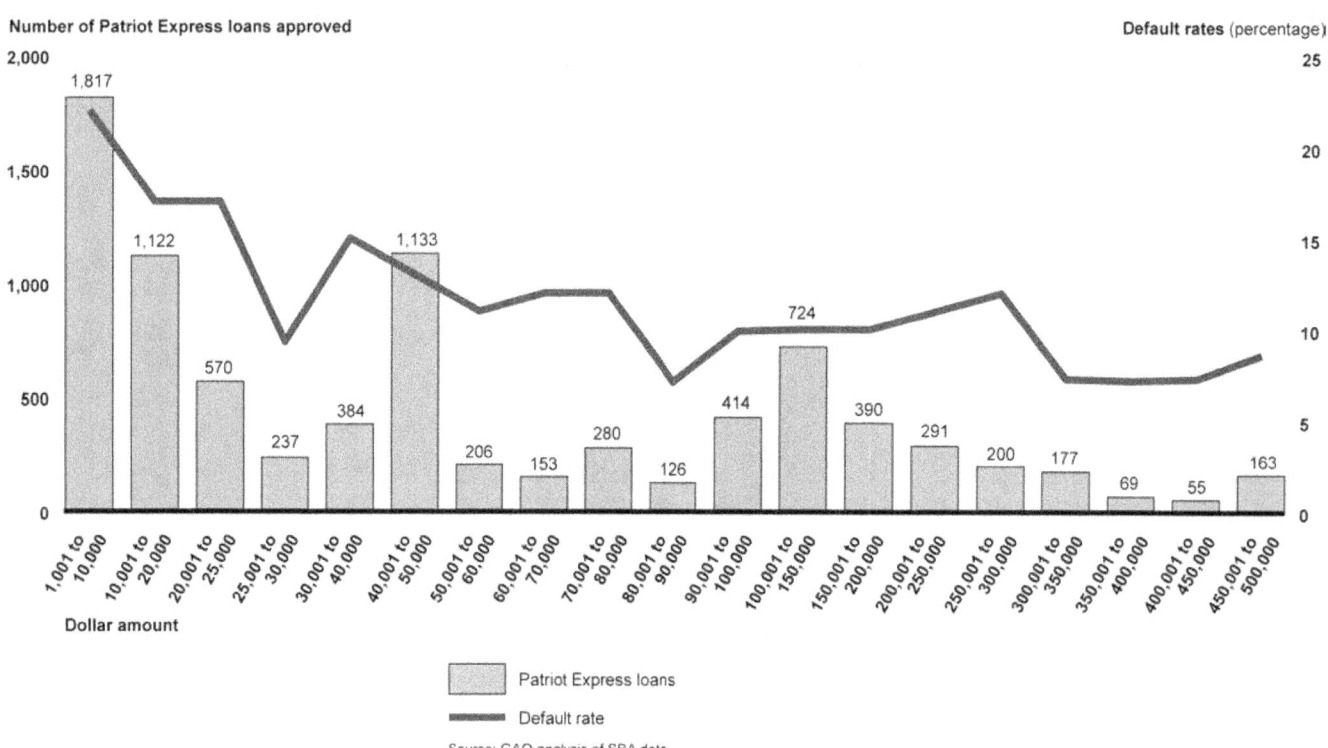

Source: GAO analysis of SBA data

Note: This figure presents default rates for Patriot Express, from 2007 to 2012. The Patriot Express program began on June 28, 2007.

Our analysis of SBA data identified a concentration of low-dollar, uncollateralized Patriot Express loans with significantly higher default rates (compared to other Patriot Express loans) that were approved by a single lender. In 2009, the peak year for Patriot Express, this lender accounted for about 39 percent of Patriot Express loans approved, as shown in figure 8. Patriot Express loans approved by this lender have been defaulting at rates as high as 38 percent for loans approved in 2008 and 25 percent for loans approved in 2009, approximately 13 percentage points higher than loans approved by other lenders in the same years, also shown in figure 8. Although overall default rates have decreased since 2008, the default rates for this lender remain significantly higher than those of all other lenders. For example, in 2009, at 25 percent, the default rate of the one lender was more than double that of the remaining lenders, at 12 percent. In May 2013, SBA decided not to renew this lender's delegated authority to make SBA loans, which includes its authority to make Patriot Express loans.

Figure 8: Total Number of Patriot Express Loans and Default Rates by Lender and Loan Approval Year 2007-2012, as of December 31, 2012

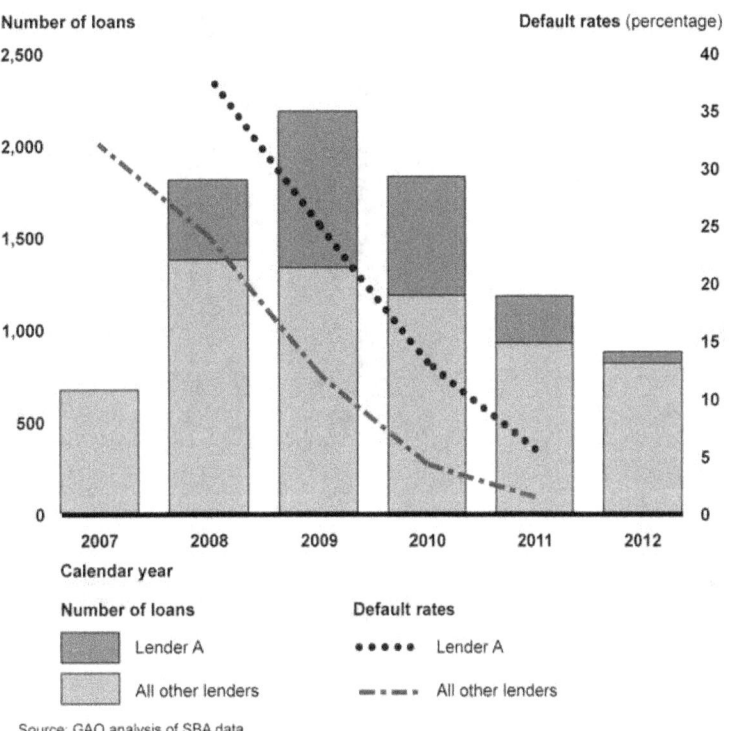

Source: GAO analysis of SBA data.

Note: We did not include the default rate for loans approved in 2012 because too little time has passed as of December 31, 2012, to fully assess the default rate for this cohort. The Patriot Express program began on June 28, 2007.

Figure 9 shows the default rates of Patriot Express, SBA Express, and 7(a) by loan amounts. When comparing default rates with different loan amounts based on program requirements, the performance of Patriot Express loans improves as loan amounts increase. For example, the largest improvement in performance for Patriot Express loans was between loans of less than $25,000 and loans valued from $25,000 to $150,000; for loans in this range, the default rate drops by almost half, from 20 percent to 12 percent. As mentioned earlier, more than 64 percent of loans up to $25,000 were provided by one lender. However, even when loans approved by this one lender were excluded, the default rate for loans up to $25,000 did not change significantly.

Figure 9: Default Rates by Loan Amounts Approved for Patriot Express, SBA Express, and 7(a), 2007-2012

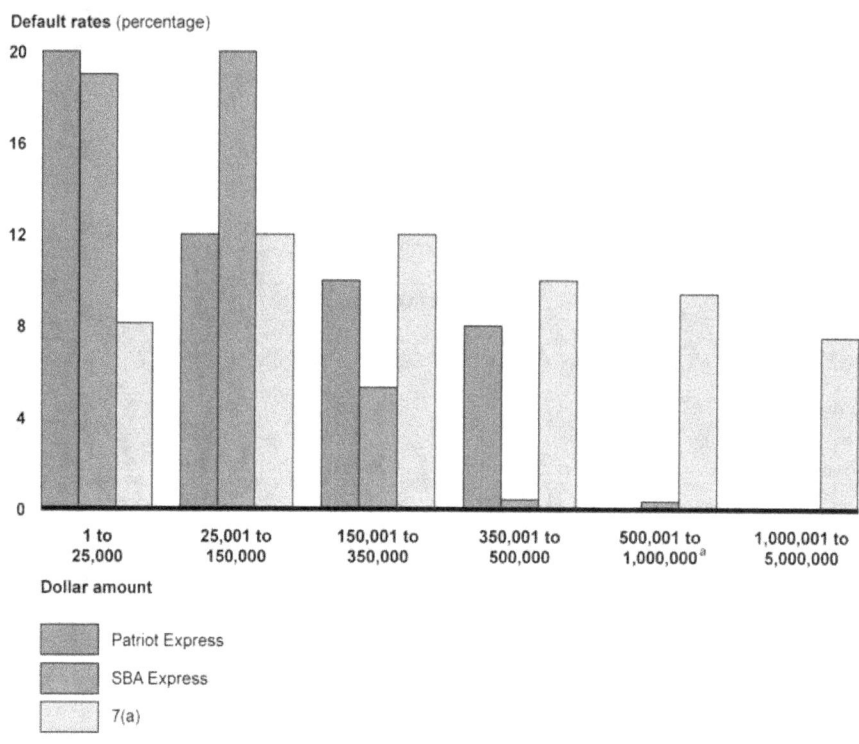

Source: GAO analysis of SBA data.

Note: This figure presents default rates for Patriot Express, SBA Express, and 7(a) from 2007-2012. The Patriot Express program began on June 28, 2007. In the figure, we present 2007 default rates for the entire year for the 7(a) and SBA Express programs. Limiting our analysis to June 1, 2007, for Patriot Express and July 1, 2007, for 7(a) and SBA Express, produced similar results. These loan categories were chosen based on characteristics of each of the programs. For example, the first category was chosen because SBA Express and Patriot Express loans of $25,000 or less do not require collateral. The third and fourth loan categories were chosen because they were the maximum loan limits for SBA Express ($350,000) and Patriot Express ($500,000).

[a]SBA was provided authority under the Small Business Jobs Act of 2010 to raise the limit on SBA Express to $1 million for loans for 1 year following the act's enactment on September 27, 2010.

Loans to Veterans through Patriot Express, SBA Express, and 7(a) Have Declined over Time

Consistent with overall SBA lending through Patriot Express, SBA Express, and 7(a), available data suggest that the number of loans made to veterans through these programs are currently at similar levels, but overall lending to veterans through these programs has decreased over the past 8 years. Although some SBA loans made to veterans may not be identified, the available data using the veteran status field in SBA's database show that the differences in levels of lending to veterans across the 7(a), SBA Express, and Patriot Express programs have been lower over the last 2 years, as shown in figure 10. For example, in 2012, 664 loans were made to veterans through the Patriot Express program, 551 loans through the SBA Express program, and 391 loans through the 7(a) program. In comparison, there were more than twice as many Patriot Express loans made to veterans compared to SBA Express loans and 7(a) loans in 2009.[19] The trends shown in figure 10 are consistent with overall lending from 2007 through 2012 in terms of total loans made under Patriot Express, SBA Express, and 7(a).

[19]The SBA loan-level data for these three programs include a field that indicates whether a loan has been made to a veteran, service-disabled veteran, or Vietnam War veteran. However, unlike borrowers in the Patriot Express program—which requires lenders to confirm a veteran's status for eligibility purposes—veterans who receive 7(a) or SBA Express loans self-report their veteran status to SBA, and the lender is not required to verify this information. Because this information is self-reported, SBA officials indicated that the veteran status field for 7(a) and SBA Express borrowers may not be accurately or consistently capturing all veterans who have received a loan through these programs.

Figure 10: Number of Patriot Express, SBA Express, and 7(a) Loans Made to Veterans, 2001-2012

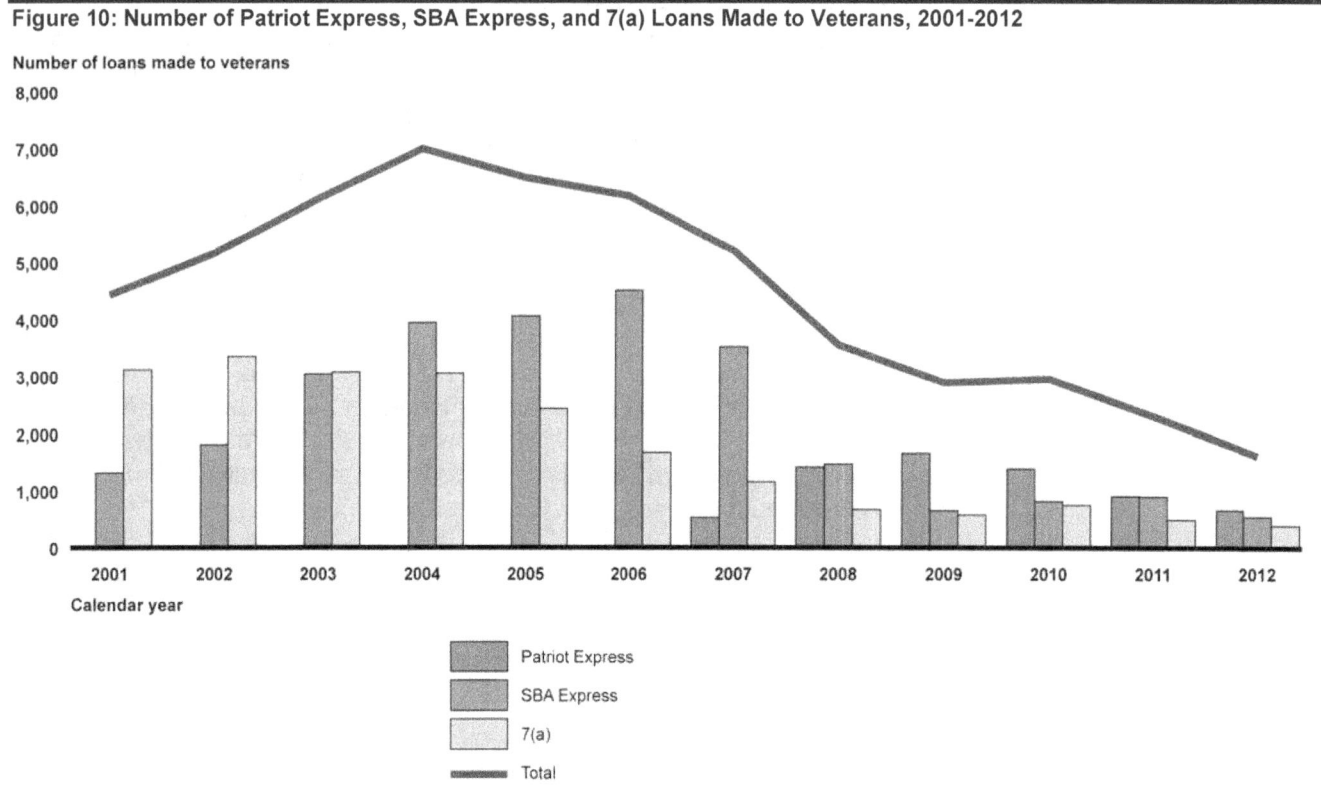

Number of loans made to veterans

Calendar year

- Patriot Express
- SBA Express
- 7(a)
- Total

Source: GAO analysis of SBA data.

Note: The Patriot Express program began on June 28, 2007. Because this information is self-reported, SBA officials indicated that the veteran status field in its database for 7(a) and SBA Express borrowers may not be accurately or consistently capturing all veterans who have received a loan through these programs. The numbers for 2001-2006 are based on data provided by SBA, while the numbers for 2007-2012 are based on our analysis of SBA data.

Although veterans have been able to access capital through the Patriot Express, SBA Express, and 7(a) loan programs, overall lending to veterans peaked in 2004—at which time only the 7(a) and SBA Express programs existed—and has continued to decrease since then, even after the Patriot Express program started in 2007. Between 2004 and 2012, the number of loans made to veterans decreased 77 percent, from about 7,000 loans in 2004 to 1,600 loans in 2012. Further, even with the introduction of the Patriot Express program in 2007, the overall levels of lending to veterans through all three SBA programs has remained lower than the overall level of lending to veterans before the program's inception. A number of factors could have contributed to this decrease in overall lending to veterans through SBA programs, including more conservative lender credit standards and the economic downturn in 2008.

GAO-13-727 SBA Patriot Express

In addition, as mentioned previously, veteran status information is self-reported by 7(a) and SBA Express borrowers, and the veteran status field may not accurately and consistently capture all veterans who have received a loan through these programs.

In addition to a decrease in the total number of loans, the total dollar amount of loans made to veterans through Patriot Express, SBA Express, and 7(a) and also decreased from 2007 through 2012. As shown in figure 11, the overall dollar amount of loans to veterans through these three programs decreased from 2007 through 2009 before spiking in 2010 and continuing to decline again through 2012.[20] The trends shown in figure 11 are consistent with overall lending in terms of total value of loans made under the Patriot Express, SBA Express, and 7(a) programs from 2007 through 2012. In May 2013, SBA announced a new initiative to increase lending to veteran entrepreneurs by $475 million over the next 5 years across all SBA loan programs.

---

[20]As mentioned earlier, the higher number of 7(a) and Patriot Express loans approved in 2009 and 2010 may be attributable, in part, to ARRA and subsequent legislation, which provided funding to temporarily subsidize the 7(a) guarantee programs' fees and to increase the programs' maximum loan guarantee percentage from 75 or 85 percent to 90 percent.

Figure 11: Dollar Amounts Approved for Patriot Express, SBA Express, and 7(a) Loans Made to Veterans, 2007-2012

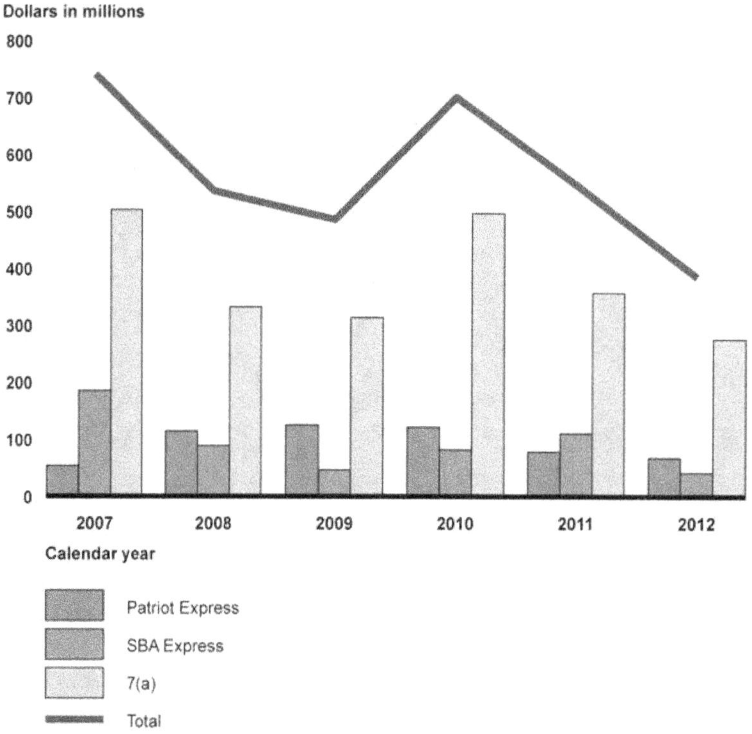

Source: GAO analysis of SBA data.

Note: The Patriot Express program began on June 28, 2007.

Figure 12 shows the default rates of Patriot Express, SBA Express, and 7(a) loans made to veterans by approval year. Loans made to veterans through these programs in 2007 and 2008 had higher default rates than those in more recent years, which may be at least partially explained by the longer time periods these loans have had in which to observe defaults. While the default rates for veteran loans for SBA Express and 7(a) have decreased for more recent loan cohorts, the Patriot Express default rates for veteran loans remained relatively high. For example, Patriot Express loans made to veterans in 2009 and 2010 defaulted more than twice as often as loans made to veterans through SBA Express and 7(a).

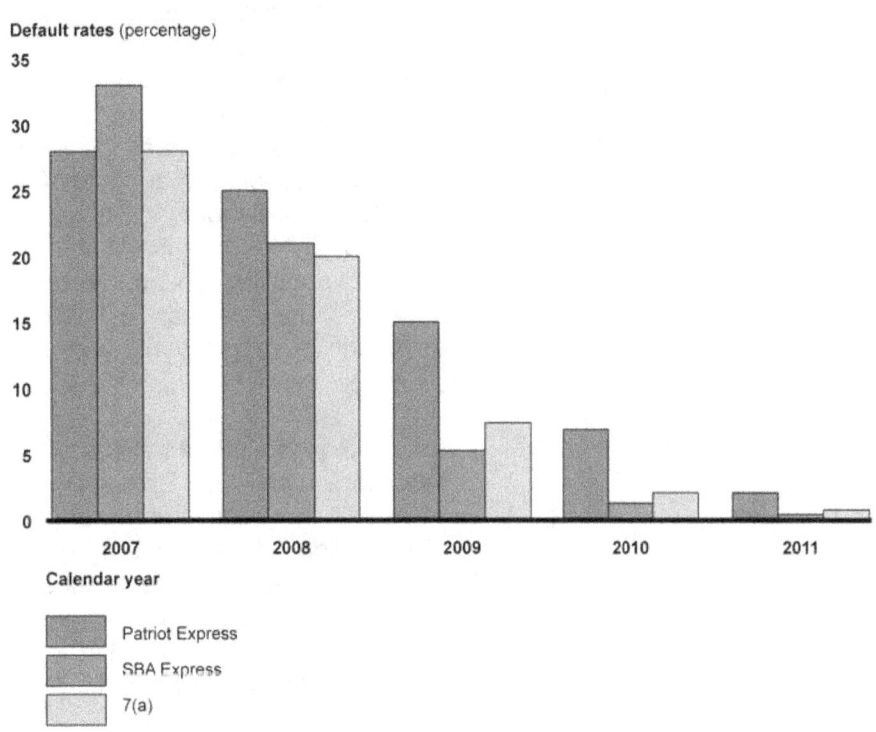

Figure 12: Default Rates of Loans Made to Veterans through Patriot Express, SBA Express, and 7(a) by Year of Approval, as of December 31, 2012

Default rates (percentage)

Calendar year

- Patriot Express
- SBA Express
- 7(a)

Source: GAO analysis of SBA data.

Note: We did not include the default rate for loans approved in 2012 because too little time has passed as of December 31, 2012, to fully assess the default rate for this cohort. The Patriot Express program began on June 28, 2007. In the figure, we present 2007 default rates for the entire year for the 7(a) and SBA Express programs. Limiting our analysis to July 1, 2007, for Patriot Express, SBA Express, and 7(a) produced similar results.

Patriot Express Costs Exceed Fees Collected and Recoveries

According to our analysis of SBA's data on Patriot Express, program costs exceed the fees collected, funds recovered from borrowers in default, and other funds collected by SBA to offset the costs of the program. SBA's costs for the Patriot Express program are primarily based on the guaranteed portion of the purchased loan. As described earlier, when a loan defaults, the lender asks SBA to honor the guarantee (that is, purchase the loan). For the Patriot Express program, as indicated previously, the guaranteed portion is 85 percent for loans of $150,000 or less and 75 percent for loans over $150,000.[21] The exact amount that SBA purchases is offset by any proceeds of sale of collateral prior to purchase. Following default, if SBA determines that it will honor the guarantee, SBA purchases these loans from the lender at either 85 percent or 75 percent, depending on the approved value of the loan.[22] These costs are partially offset by guarantee fees that SBA collects at origination and annual fees it collects from lenders. Additional offsets are based on recoveries in the form of borrower payments following purchase or from proceeds from the liquidation of collateral that was not liquidated within 60 days following default of the loan.[23] According to SBA officials, Patriot Express lenders are required to liquidate non-real-estate collateral prior to purchase, unless situations arise that would prevent them from liquidating, such as a bankruptcy or stay on liquidation.[24] In these situations, SBA will purchase a loan prior to full liquidation.

As shown in table 3, from fiscal years 2007 through 2012, SBA purchased $45.3 million in Patriot Express loans. These default costs were offset by $12.9 million in collected fees and $1.3 million in recoveries, resulting in $31.1 million in losses for this period (excluding future revenues from fees and potential additional recoveries). Based on these cash flows, the Patriot Express program has had an overall recovery rate of 2.87 percent since 2008—that is, of $45.3 million in Patriot Express loans that SBA purchased from 2008 through 2012, SBA has recovered almost $1.3

---

[21]As indicated earlier, the guarantee was increased to 90 percent as part of ARRA and subsequent legislation for 7(a) loans made from February 17, 2009, through March 4, 2011.

[22]According to SBA guidance, the guarantee portion of the loan is 85 percent for loans of $150,000 or less, and 75 percent for loans above $150,000.

[23]As stated earlier in figure 2, according to SBA, for loans approved on or after May 14, 2007, a lender may demand in writing that SBA honor its guarantee if the borrower is in default on any installment for more than 60 calendar days and the default has not been cured, provided all business personal property securing the defaulted SBA loan has been liquidated.

[24]As mentioned earlier, SBA considers liquidation of business personal property collateral to be complete when a lender has exhausted all prudent and commercially reasonable efforts to collect upon those assets.

million (2.87 percent) of the funds.[25] The low recovery rate for Patriot Express makes it more likely that the program will continue operating at a loss. In addition, SBA provided projected cash flows for the Patriot Express program, which show projected losses of $36 million including future revenues from fees and potential recoveries.

Table 3: Patriot Express Program Fees, Recoveries, Purchases, and Net Cash Flows, Fiscal Years 2007-2012

Fiscal year	Up-front fee	Annual fee	Recovery	Purchase	Net cash flow[a]
2007	$338,274	$122	N/A	N/A	$338,397
2008	2,621,719	218,692	$4,077	- $275,603	2,568,884
2009	1,083,855	661,610	4,058	- 3,589,587	- 1,840,063
2010	657,255	1,124,399	219,147	- 12,800,709	- 10,799,908
2011	1,273,529	1,495,612	439,620	- 15,626,195	- 12,417,434
2012	1,903,299	1,518,379	631,337	- 13,004,418	- 8,951,403
Total	**$7,877,931**	**$5,018,815**	**$1,298,239**	**- $45,296,512**	**-$31,101,527**

Source: SBA.

Note: Totals for each column may not add up exactly due to rounding.

[a]Net cash flow is equal to the sum of all fees and recoveries minus purchases.

Figure 13 shows SBA's loan purchases compared to the funds collected to offset those costs, including both fees and recoveries. Purchases peaked in 2011 and then declined slightly, but have remained significantly higher than the offsets.

---

[25]The estimated recovery rate was calculated from 2008 because no recoveries or purchases occurred in 2007. The recovery rate is calculated by dividing the total of all recoveries from 2008 to 2012 by the total purchases for the same time period. Recoveries include proceeds from the sale of any collateral attached to the loan at the time of purchase, including other payments from the borrower following purchase.

GAO-13-727 SBA Patriot Express

Figure 13: Patriot Express Purchases and Offsets, Fiscal Years 2007-2012

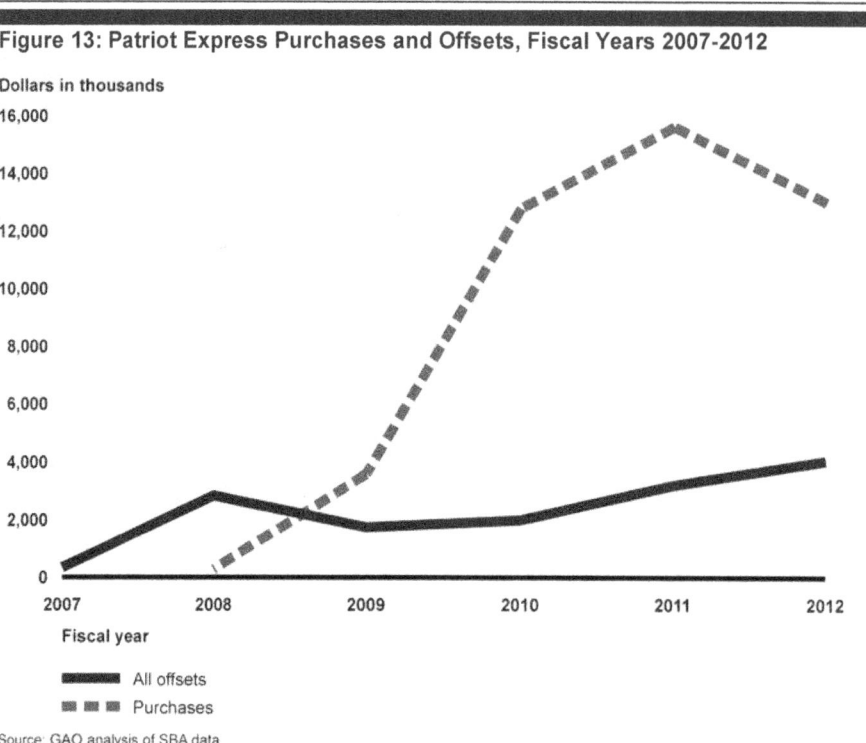

Dollars in thousands

All offsets
Purchases

Source: GAO analysis of SBA data.

Given the losses in the Patriot Express program since inception, if the program continues on its current trend, Patriot Express costs will likely continue to exceed fees collected and recoveries. In a program that currently has high defaults and relatively small recoveries, SBA faces challenges in taking in offsets sufficient to cover the costs of the program. Recoveries are particularly limited in loans of a low-dollar value (below $25,000) because no collateral is attached to these loans. As discussed earlier, 41.2 percent of all Patriot Express loans were for amounts less than $25,000, and 21.3 percent were for amounts less than $10,000.

Another factor that may affect the net cost of the Patriot Express program is the extent to which SBA has been making improper payments—that is, making guarantee payments that should not have been made—on Patriot

Express loans.[26] According to SBA, the improper payment review for 7(a) includes loans made under the Patriot Express program. In November 2012, the SBA Office of Inspector General (OIG) calculated that the improper payment rate for the 7(a) program could be as high as 20 percent, a significantly higher rate than SBA reports (about 2 percent).[27] According to OIG officials, some of the reasons that SBA did not identify improper payments were that its reviewers were unfamiliar with or misinterpreted agency policies or did not have sufficient time to conduct improper payment reviews. The SBA OIG's higher estimated rate could indicate that SBA is paying more than is necessary on defaulted loans in the 7(a) program, including the Patriot Express program. The SBA OIG found that SBA did not detect all improper payments when conducting improper payment reviews to estimate its fiscal year 2011 improper payment rate for 7(a) guarantee purchases. From a sample of 303 guarantee purchases made between April 1, 2010, and March 31, 2011, originally selected by SBA, the SBA OIG sampled 30 purchases for improper payment review and determined that SBA did not detect 6 loans that were purchased improperly.[28] Although SBA disagreed with the OIG's assessment, SBA acknowledged that the improper payment rate could be as high as close to 10 percent. OIG reviewed and reaffirmed its original methodology as an accurate assessment of SBA's real improper payment rate and concluded that the rate could potentially be as high as 20 percent.[29] The SBA OIG made 12 recommendations to SBA, including that SBA create more comprehensive guidance and policies to better detect improper payments, provide training for SBA staff to conduct

---

[26]When a loan goes into default and the lender requests guarantee payment from SBA, SBA reviews loan documentation to evaluate the lender's compliance with program rules and regulations to justify the guarantee purchase. According to Office of Management and Budget (OMB) guidance, an improper payment is any payment that should not have been made or that was made in an incorrect amount under statutory, contractual, administrative, or other legally applicable requirement.

[27]SBA, Office of Inspector General, *The Small Business Administration's Improper Payment Rate for 7(a) Guaranty Purchases Remains Significantly Underestimated*, Report No. 13-07 (Washington, D.C.: Nov. 15, 2012).

[28]According to the OIG audit, the OIG's statistician tested the sampling methodology used by SBA and the OIG to ensure it would produce a statistically valid estimate of the rate of improper payments.

[29]In response to SBA's written response stating that OIG's estimated improper payment rate was based on a flawed statistical approach, OIG noted that it would be extremely unlikely—1 chance in 1.72 million—that the deficiencies would only exist in the subsample of 30 and nowhere else.

reviews, and determine the appropriate amount of time needed for loan reviews to better identify erroneous payments. The SBA OIG indicated that SBA is making progress on these recommendations.

Finally, according to SBA officials, administrative costs directly associated with Patriot Express are minimal because they have no dedicated staff for Patriot Express. The only unique administrative costs they have dedicated to the program were those involved in creating it in 2007. These officials reported that SBA is able to administer the program using existing staff and resources dedicated to 7(a) and SBA Express programs and there are no separate line items for administrative costs for Patriot Express. SBA's administrative expenses for fiscal year 2012 for all business loan programs (which includes Patriot Express) were $148 million.

Stakeholders Reported Benefits and Challenges, but SBA Has Not Evaluated the Effects of the Patriot Express Pilot

Selected loan recipients and lenders, as well as veteran service organizations we met with, identified various benefits and challenges to Patriot Express, but SBA has not evaluated the effects of the Patriot Express pilot. Lenders and borrowers we met with most frequently identified supporting veteran businesses and providing veterans with a streamlined application process as benefits of the program. Low awareness among veterans of the program and participating lenders were among the most frequently cited challenges by selected lenders, borrowers, and veteran service organizations. In addition to Patriot Express, veterans also access capital through alternate SBA-guaranteed loan products and other means. SBA provides optional training and counseling through a variety of resources to help veteran entrepreneurs navigate the options available to them. However, as with some of its previous pilot loan programs, SBA has not conducted an evaluation of the Patriot Express program to assess the extent to which it is achieving its objectives, including an assessment of its effect on eligible borrowers. Our previous work has shown that an evaluation gives an agency the opportunity to refine the design of a program and determine whether program operations have resulted in the desired benefits for participants.

Helping Veterans Expand Their Business and Providing a Streamlined Loan Process Were among the Cited Benefits of the Program

Participating loan recipients and lenders, as well as veteran service organizations we met with, identified supporting veteran businesses as a top benefit of the Patriot Express program. Specifically, 21 of the 24 Patriot Express loan recipients we met with said that the loan had enabled them to start their business, expand operations, or keep their business open during challenging times. In addition, four of the six recipients we spoke with who received a line of credit through the program said that having available credit increased their attractiveness as a potential contractor because it signaled to other businesses that they could pay for the costs to complete projects. Ten loan recipients believed that if they had not received the loan, they would currently not be in business because the loan provided capital at a critical point in time. The remaining 14 loan recipients believed that they would still be in business if they had not received the loan but would have faced difficult decisions to cover the costs, including firing staff and foregoing key projects. All loan recipients we met with said that they would apply for the program again based on their experience, and 6 recipients had pursued and received another Patriot Express loan. Likewise, the three veteran service organizations that we met with stated that the program benefited veterans who obtained Patriot Express loans.

The Patriot Express program provides veterans with a streamlined application process, and loan recipients and lenders we met with noted that this was a benefit of the program. Six of the eight lenders and one veteran service organization we met with said that the program provided veterans with a less onerous application process and reduced SBA paperwork requirements, particularly when compared to SBA's 7(a) loan program. For example, SBA requires borrowers to submit additional documents to apply for a 7(a) loan, such as monthly cash-flow projections, income statements, and balance sheets for the last 3 years. Further, since 7(a) borrowers must pledge all available collateral up to the loan amount, SBA requires borrowers to complete a schedule of collateral of all real estate and personal property used to secure the loan and provide supporting documents for such collateral, including real estate appraisals and environmental investigation reports.[30] Almost all loan

---

[30]Patriot Express loans of less than $25,000 do not require collateral and lenders may use their own collateral policies for their nonguaranteed loans for Patriot Express loans over $25,000 but below $350,000. For loans greater than $350,000, the lender must take all available collateral up to the loan amount. As mentioned previously, 41.2 percent of Patriot Express loans made since the program's inception were less than $25,000 and are, therefore, uncollateralized.

recipients we met with reported that they had a positive experience with the Patriot Express loan application process, including satisfaction with the amount of documentation required. In addition, nearly all loan recipients said that they received the loan proceeds in a timely manner, ranging from a few days to 3 months from the time they applied for the loan.

Selected loan recipients, lenders, and veteran service organizations also identified other benefits to the program, such as providing veterans with favorable loan terms. For example, nearly all lenders, one veteran service organization, and officials from the National Association of Government Guaranteed Lenders (NAGGL) said that the program provided veterans with more favorable loan terms than an SBA Express loan, such as lower interest rates or higher maximum loan amounts.[31] In addition, seven loan recipients we met with said that the Patriot Express loan terms provided a more cost-effective credit alternative to fund their small business expenses compared to other financing options. For instance, four recipients stated that receiving a Patriot Express loan saved them from using credit cards and other expensive lines of credit to obtain the necessary capital for their business.

Finally, borrowers, lenders, and veteran service organizations we met with said that having a dedicated program solely for those in the military community was a benefit. For example, 10 Patriot Express loan recipients said that they appreciated that the program targeted veterans specifically and noted that it played a large role in their decision to obtain the loan. In addition, one lender said that having a loan program that also targets the business needs of spouses of service members or reservists is valuable, particularly if the business is jointly owned by the couple, because it provides access to capital to expand the business if one spouse is deployed. Further, two veteran service organizations we met with stressed that having a program for veterans also helped to initiate conversations between the veteran entrepreneur and the lender about other small business resources and financing options available.

---

[31]NAGGL is a trade organization that represents SBA 7(a) lenders.

Low Awareness of the Program and Its Participating Lenders Were Reported as Challenges, among Others

Lack of Awareness of the Program

Selected loan recipients, lenders, and veteran service organizations said that a low awareness of the Patriot Express program among the military community was among the most frequently cited challenges. Specifically, over half of the Patriot Express loan recipients, six of the eight lenders, and two veteran service organizations we met with said that SBA could do more to increase outreach to veteran entrepreneurs and better market the program to the military community. In addition, five loan recipients did not know about the program until they approached a lender for financing and were notified about it. Further, awareness of the program among selected veteran entrepreneurs who have not participated in the program was also low. For example, 11 of the 16 veterans that received 7(a) loans and all 15 SBA Express veteran loan recipients that we were able to contact were unaware that Patriot Express existed.[32]

SBA officials said the agency tries to increase awareness of the program through district offices, resource partners, and lenders. For example, SBA officials noted that there is a veteran loan specialist at each SBA district office who could recommend specific small business resources, including the Patriot Express program, to veteran entrepreneurs. Additionally, SBA officials said that their resource partners, such as Small Business Development Centers (SBDC) and SCORE (formerly the Service Corps of Retired Executives) chapters, could advertise the program through hosted events that discuss potential options for financing small business needs. Five loan recipients we met with said that they learned about the program through an SBA resource partner, including SBDCs and SCORE counselors, and two noted that these resources further helped them to find a participating lender. For example, one loan recipient said that the SBDC staff member who told him about the program also recommended a lender, assisted him with his loan application, and followed up with him after the loan was approved.

---

[32]In addition to the 24 Patriot Express loan recipients, we attempted to contact veterans who were aware of the program and have received SBA 7(a) and SBA Express loans. As part of our attempt to contact these veterans, we found that some were not aware of the Patriot Express program, and we did not interview them as part of our review.

SBA officials also said that they have reached out to NAGGL to increase marketing of the program at the lender level. According to NAGGL officials, NAGGL hosted roundtables at its 2013 Lender Leadership Summit and Lending Technical Conference to discuss ways that lenders can better serve veteran entrepreneurs, including the Patriot Express program. Although NAGGL does not participate in marketing SBA programs to borrowers, NAGGL officials said that individual lenders typically advertise certain SBA loans based on their involvement with those programs. For example, some lenders we met with noted that they try to increase awareness by marketing themselves as Patriot Express lenders, particularly if they have branches in locations with large concentrations of veterans. These lenders also partnered with veteran groups at their branch locations and presented their loan products, including Patriot Express loans, to interested members at events hosted by veteran groups. One lender, however, noted that it was difficult to market SBA loan products at their branches because identifying borrowers who can qualify for SBA loans can be challenging. According to this lender, pursuant to SBA's "credit elsewhere" requirement, the lender needs to first evaluate a borrower's ability to obtain credit against their own lending policies for conventional loans in order to determine if an SBA loan product is appropriate for the borrower.[33] This approach is consistent with what we have previously reported regarding how lenders make credit elsewhere decisions.[34]

Low Awareness among Borrowers of Participating Lenders

Patriot Express and 7(a) loan recipients we met with stated that low awareness of which lenders make Patriot Express loans is also a challenge to the program. For example, 7 of the 24 Patriot Express recipients and 3 of the 4 7(a) veteran loan recipients we met with reported that SBA could provide better information about which lenders currently participate in the program. A majority of these 10 recipients found that the search for a participating lender was difficult and required many phone calls and visits to lenders. Three recipients also noted that the SBA resources they used incorrectly identified banks as participating lenders. For example, one veteran said that he spent significant time away from his business to contact six banks—which the district SBA office said were

---

[33]For purposes of this report, a conventional loan is a loan without a federal guarantee.

[34]GAO, *Small Business Administration: Additional Guidance on Documenting Credit Elsewhere Decisions Could Improve 7(a) Program Oversight*, GAO-09-228 (Washington D.C.: Feb. 12, 2009).

participating lenders—and found that none of them participated in Patriot Express. Additionally, two 7(a) veteran loan recipients said they initially sought financing through the Patriot Express program but they said that they settled for a 7(a) loan when they could not find a participating lender. Further, two Patriot Express loan recipients told us that they paid fees to a third-party entity that could identify lenders that made Patriot Express loans. All 10 of these recipients stated that having a consolidated and up-to-date list of participating lenders would have been helpful to their search for a loan.

SBA officials said that they did not have a list of participating lenders on their website because the agency did not want to appear to be steering borrowers toward financing their businesses through loans, especially loans from particular lenders. Rather, SBA officials stated that prospective veteran borrowers interested in the program should first contact an SBA district office or SBDC to determine if financing through a loan would be suitable for their business. Further, SBA officials said that if financing through a loan was the best solution for the veteran, SBDCs would then give the veteran a list of local lenders that participate in the program. As mentioned previously, two of the loan recipients we met with found a lender through these SBA resources, such as SBDCs and SCORE counselors.

Other Challenges

Other challenges reported by selected borrowers, lenders, and veteran service organizations included high fees associated with the loan, stringent collateral requirements, and limited maximum loan amount.

- *High Fees*: Six Patriot Express loan recipients and five lenders we met with said that the SBA guarantee fees were unaffordable for some veterans and suggested that they should be reduced or waived. These six Patriot Express loan recipients also noted that the lender packaging fees were unaffordable and suggested that they should be reduced or waived as well. According to SBA officials, the guarantee fee plays an important role in the continuation of the loan guarantee program because fees are collected to offset potential losses from defaulted and purchased loans. SBA officials also noted that the guarantee fee is ultimately the responsibility of the lender, though often it is passed on to the borrower.[35] In addition, SBA guidance establishes limits to the amount of packaging and other fees a lender can charge based on a percentage of the loan amount.[36] SBA officials said that issues regarding potentially excessive fees charged at origination could be identified either through complaints from the SBA OIG's hotline or during SBA's 7(a) lender on-site examinations, which are discussed in the next section of this report. According to SBA officials, there has only been one complaint about fees, which was reported to the SBA OIG hotline. SBA officials said they resolved the issue by confirming that the fees were inconsistent with SBA guidance and working with the lender to compensate the borrower.

- *Stringent Collateral Requirements*: Three Patriot Express loan recipients noted that they struggled to meet the collateral requirements for their loans.[37] Additionally, three lenders felt that the SBA collateral requirement for Patriot Express loans above $350,000—for which the borrower must make all collateral available to the lender up to the loan amount— was excessive and a disincentive for prospective veteran borrowers to participate in the program. According to SBA officials, the agency is considering some modifications to the collateral requirements for regular 7(a) that would still maintain a strong underwriting process. To the extent those changes are adopted, they would apply as well to Patriot Express loans in excess of $350,000.

- *Limited Maximum Loan Amount*: Two Patriot Express loan recipients, two veteran service organizations, and one lender we met with said

---

[35]The President's 2014 budget waives guarantee fees on loans of less than $150,000 in SBA's 7(a) loan program, including the Patriot Express program. However, existing fees on loans $150,000 and greater will remain, and SBA's budget would need to be adjusted accordingly in order to offset the fees that would have been collected from loans less than $150,000.

[36]SBA SOP-51-10 5(E) states that packaging and other fees must be consistent with those charged on the lender's similarly sized, non-SBA-guaranteed loans. For more information on maximum allowable fees, see appendix II.

[37]SBA's collateral policies for Patriot Express loans vary depending on the loan amount. For example, no collateral is required for Patriot Express loans of less than $25,000. On the other hand, lenders that make Patriot Express loans above $350,000 are required to collateralize the loan to the maximum extent possible up to the loan amount. If business assets do not fully secure the loan, the lender must take available personal assets of the principals as collateral. See appendix II for more information on the program's collateral policies.

that the current maximum loan amount for the program was challenging because certain projects and contracts require more than $500,000.[38] For example, one veteran service organization we met with noted that veterans who are federal contractors often need a loan for more than $500,000 to win a contract. SBA officials noted that the agency has not considered changing the maximum loan amount for Patriot Express loans.

Veterans Also Access Capital through Alternate SBA Programs and Other Means

Veterans access capital through other SBA-guaranteed loan products, including 7(a), SBA Express, and Small Loan Advantage (SLA) loans.[39] These loan products have some terms that are similar to those of Patriot Express and some that are different, as shown in figure 14.

---

[38]As previously discussed, the maximum loan amount for the Patriot Express program is $500,000.

[39]Announced in 2010, the SLA initiative was aimed at increasing lower-dollar SBA loans in underserved communities by offering lenders a prescreen credit score from SBA that the applicant's business has sufficient creditworthiness to warrant giving the applicant full consideration for financing.

Figure 14: Examples of Loan Terms for a Patriot Express, Express, 7(a), and Small Loan Advantage Loan to a Veteran Borrower

	Loan amount	SBA Guaranteed portion of loan amount	Borrower Guarantee fee	Maximum Interest rate	Monthly Payments	Target processing time	Collateral policy
Scenario 1: $10,000, 5-year loan (Prime = 3.25%)							
Patriot Express	$10,000	$ 8,500 (85%)	$170	Prime + 4.25% = 7.5%	$ 200	1 business day	No collateral required
SBA Express	10,000	5,000 (50%)	100	Prime + 6.5% = 9.75%	211	1 business day	No collateral required
7(a)	10,000	8,500 (85%)	170	Prime + 4.25% = 7.5%	200	• Regular 7(a): 6 business days • Delegated 7(a): 1 business day	All available collateral up to $10,000
SLA	10,000	8,500 (85%)	170	Prime + 4.25% = 7.5%	200	1 business day	No collateral required
Scenario 2: $250,000, 5-year loan (Prime = 3.25%)							
Patriot Express	$250,000	$ 187,500 (75%)	$5,625	Prime + 2.25% = 5.5%	$4,775	1 business day	Follow lender's collateral policy
SBA Express	250,000	125,000 (50%)	3,750	Prime + 4.5% = 7.75%	5,039	1 business day	Follow lender's collateral policy
7(a)	250,000	187,500 (75%)	5,625	Prime + 2.25% = 5.5%	4,775	• Regular 7(a): 6 business days • Delegated 7(a): 1 business day	All available collateral up to $250,000
SLA	250,000	187,500 (75%)	5,625	Prime + 2.25% = 5.5%	4,775	1 business day	Follow lender's collateral policy, but at a minimum must obtain lien on business assets of applicant
Scenario 3: $500,000 5-year loan (Prime = 3.25%)							
Patriot Express	$500,000	$375,000 (75%)	$11,250	Prime + 2.25% = 5.5%	$ 9,551	1 business day	All available collateral up to $500,000
SBA Express	Not available at this loan amount (Maximum loan amount is $350,000)						
7(a)	500,000	375,000 (75%)	11,250	Prime + 2.25% = 5.5%	9,551	• Regular 7(a): 6 business days • Delegated 7(a): 1 business day	All available collateral up to $500,000
SLA	Not available at this loan amount (Maximum loan amount is $350,000)						

Source: SBA.

Note: 7(a) loans refer to (1) regular (nondelegated) 7(a) loans and (2) delegated 7(a) loans made by lenders in the Preferred Lenders Program (PLP).

As shown above, there are several similarities and differences between the programs, and three lenders we met with reported that deciding which

SBA loan products to offer veteran borrowers was challenging. For example, Patriot Express loans offer veteran recipients lower maximum interest rates, but higher guarantee percentages and fees compared to SBA Express. Additionally, while regular 7(a) loans can provide veterans with similar loan terms and fees, these loans typically have longer processing times than Patriot Express loans due to the increased SBA paperwork requirements previously discussed. While Patriot Express and SLA have some similar loan terms, SBA officials identified other differences in the programs.[40] Three of the eight lenders we met with said that deciding what product to offer a veteran entrepreneur was difficult because the loan terms and underwriting process for a Patriot Express loan were similar to those of other SBA loans they offered. Additionally, seven of the eight lenders believed that if the Patriot Express program were not available, veterans could still access capital through these other SBA loan programs.

While 7(a) and SBA Express are alternatives to Patriot Express, loan recipients noted that other ways veterans could access capital were less advantageous and all loan recipients we met with were not aware of any veteran-specific loan guarantee programs aside from Patriot Express. For example, nine recipients said that veterans could finance their small business needs through conventional loans or credit cards, but they stated these options may be more expensive than a Patriot Express loan because they typically have higher interest rates. Two recipients considered bringing on an investor, which would inject capital into their business, but would require the recipient to give up ownership of a part of the business to the new investor. Finally, five recipients thought about financing their business through their personal savings accounts, but said that this option could have depleted their savings and a few noted that it might not have been enough to cover the amount of capital needed.

---

[40]SBA officials identified differences in the programs such as differences in the credit analysis used by the programs and the type of loan products allowed. For example, SBA officials said that lenders could use their own credit analyses for Patriot Express loans, but had to follow specific credit analysis requirements for SLA loans. Additionally, SBA officials noted that the Patriot Express program allowed revolving lines of credit, but the SLA program did not.

SBA Offers Several Veteran-Specific Training and Counseling Efforts

SBA provides training and counseling to veteran entrepreneurs through a variety of resources, although Patriot Express loan recipients are not required to use them. According to SBA officials, the agency delivers training and counseling to veterans through the following ways:

- *Cooperative agreements*: SBA has cooperative agreements with 16 organizations that serve as Veteran Business Outreach Centers (VBOC), which offer services such as business plan preparations and veteran entrepreneur counseling for service-disabled veterans. Additionally, SBA has cooperative agreements with other resource partners through which veteran entrepreneurs can receive training and counseling, including SBDCs, SCORE chapters, and Women's Business Centers (WBC). According to SBA data on veteran participation in training and counseling offered by the aforementioned resource partners (VBOCs, SBDCs, SCORE chapters, and WBCs) from fiscal year 2008 through fiscal year 2012, overall veteran participation remained steady from 2008 through 2010. However, it increased over 40 percent from approximately 115,000 veterans in 2010 to about 163,000 veterans in 2012. Further, veteran participation in training and counseling offered through VBOCs also increased in 2011, from about 45,000 veterans in 2010 to about 90,000 veterans in 2012. As of June 2013, about 36,000 veterans had received training and counseling through SCORE, SBDCs, and WBCs.[41]

- *SBA-sponsored activities*: According to SBA officials, some SBA-sponsored activities may be provided in coordination with the previously mentioned resource partners, and veterans can also receive training and counseling through these efforts. For example, Operation Boots to Business leverages SBA's resource partner network—VBOCs, SBDCs, SCORE chapters, and WBCs—and SBA's partnership with, among other entities, Syracuse University's Institute for Veterans and Military Families to provide an entrepreneurship training program for transitioning service members.[42] Operation Boots to Business consists of several phases, including a 2-day training

---

[41]Veteran participation figures in VBOCs have not yet been collected through fiscal year 2013. As of the third quarter of 2013, 28,119 veterans had been counseled and 13,619 veterans had been trained at VBOCs.

[42]The full title of the program is "Operation Boots to Business: From Service to Startup" and it was launched in 2012. Operation Boots to Business is currently in its pilot phase and is currently being tested in four Marine Corps bases before a complete national rollout to all branches of the military later in 2013.

session on creating a feasibility analysis for a business plan and an 8-week online course on the fundamentals of small business ownership, including marketing, accounting, and finance. As of March 2013, a total of 1,390 veterans (1,309 for the 2-day session and 81 for the online course) had participated in this effort.

- *SBA participation in third-party activities:* Veteran entrepreneurs can access training and counseling services provided through SBA's participation in third-party activities, including events hosted by other federal agencies and nonprofit entities. For example, SBA awarded a 3-year grant to Syracuse University to create the Entrepreneurship Bootcamp for Veterans with Disabilities (EBV), which provided small business management training to post-9/11 veterans with disabilities.[43] According to SBA, 463 veterans participated in EBV during this 3-year grant period. In 2010, SBA provided Syracuse University with funding for two additional programs that support veteran entrepreneurship: Veteran Women Igniting the Spirit of Entrepreneurship (V-WISE), which focuses on the training and mentorship of women veterans and spouses, and Operation Endure and Grow (OEG), which features an 8-week online course geared toward National Guard and Reserve members, their families, and their business partners.[44] As of April 2013, 857 women veterans, female spouses and partners of active service members, and transitioning female members of the military community had participated in V-WISE, and 168 reservists had received training through OEG.

Veterans who have participated in certain training and counseling efforts have generally found them to be helpful. For example, SBA's Office of Veterans Business Development (OVBD) conducts an annual VBOC client satisfaction survey, which shows that client satisfaction with VBOC services had increased from 85 percent in 2008 to 93 percent in 2012.[45] According to these SBA officials, the survey results are used to, among other things, identify areas for improvement and new training topics. OVBD officials said they are responsible for collecting feedback surveys

---

[43]The 3-year grant period began on November 11, 2009, and was terminated on November 10, 2012.

[44]The funding period for the V-WISE and OEG grant ends on September 30, 2013.

[45]The Office of Veterans Business Development's mission is to maximize the availability, applicability, and usability of all SBA small business programs for veterans, service-disabled veterans, reserve component members, and their dependents or survivors.

for the VBOC program only. Veterans whom we met with who participated in these efforts also found them to be helpful. Specifically, 14 of the 28 loan recipients we met with—Patriot Express loan recipients as well as 7(a) veteran loan recipients—participated in an SBA-sponsored training or counseling session, and the most commonly used resources among these recipients were SBDCs and SCORE counselors. Eight of the recipients said these sessions were helpful in starting and growing their business, such as assisting in the development of business plans and marketing strategies, and they noted that these sessions were free. Two loan recipients suggested that SBA develop more advanced workshops for seasoned entrepreneurs, but acknowledged that these training and counseling resources would be helpful for first-time business owners.

As with Some of Its Previous Pilot Programs, SBA Has Not Evaluated Patriot Express

SBA has not evaluated the Patriot Express program's performance or its effect on eligible borrowers. GAO's guide for designing evaluations states that an evaluation gives an agency the opportunity to refine the design of a program and provides a useful tool to determine whether program operations have resulted in the desired benefits for participants.[46] In addition, evaluations can inform future program decisions. Program evaluations are individual, systematic studies that use research methods to assess how well a program, operation, or project is achieving its objectives and the reasons why it may or may not be performing as expected.[47] Program evaluations are distinct from routine monitoring or performance measurement activities in that performance measurement entails the ongoing monitoring of a program's progress, whereas program evaluation typically assesses the achievement of a program's objectives and other aspects of performance in the context in which the program operates.[48] At a minimum, a well-developed and documented program evaluation plan includes measurable objectives, standards for performance, methods for data collection, and time frames for completion.

[46]GAO, *Designing Evaluations: 2012 Revision*, GAO-12-208G (Washington D.C.: Jan. 31, 2012).

[47]GAO, *Managing for Results: 2013 Federal Managers Survey on Organizational Performance and Management Issues*, GAO-13-519SP (an E-supplement to GAO-13-518) (Washington D.C.: June 26, 2013).

[48]GAO, *Program Evaluation: Strategies to Facilitate Agencies' Use of Evaluation in Program Management and Policy Making*, GAO-13-570 (Washington D.C.: June 26, 2013).

Page 2   GAO-13-727 SBA Patriot Express

Incorporating these elements and executing the plan can help ensure that the implementation of a pilot generates performance information needed to make effective management decisions about the future of the program. In addition, recent legislation has highlighted the importance of program evaluation for federal agencies. Specifically, Congress updated the Government Performance and Results Act of 1993 (GPRA) with the GPRA Modernization Act of 2010 (GPRAMA), which requires agencies to describe program evaluations that were used to establish or revise strategic goals.[49]

When Patriot Express was created in 2007 under SBA's authority to initiate pilots, SBA indicated that it would evaluate the program's performance and make a decision whether to modify or continue the program after December 31, 2010. In December 2010, SBA announced through a Federal Register notice that it would extend the pilot through 2013 in order to have more time to evaluate the effect of the program and determine whether any changes need to be made.[50] According to SBA officials, they have not established any measurable goals for the pilot, but have begun to hold meetings on what information they will need to assess the performance of Patriot Express loans. However, although SBA officials said that they have begun to hold meetings, the program extension ends in only a few months on December 31, 2013. As of August 2013, SBA had not established a plan for the evaluation of the program, and such a plan should include clear and measurable objectives, standards for performance, methods for data collection, and time frames for completion. In addition, SBA has taken several actions in an attempt to increase lending to veterans across its programs, but these initiatives have not been substantiated by findings from an evaluation of the Patriot Express program or the current state of SBA lending to veterans.

As mentioned previously, SBA announced a new initiative to increase loans to veteran entrepreneurs by $475 million over the next 5 years across all SBA loan programs. Because SBA had not conducted an evaluation of the pilot, the agency had little information available to inform such decisions, such as a comparison of benefits that veterans receive from Patriot Express in relation to those received by veterans participating

---

[49]Pub. L. No. 111-352, 124 Stat. 3866 (2011).

[50]75 Fed. Reg. 77935 (Dec. 14, 2010).

in other SBA loan programs. SBA has conducted performance measurement and monitoring activities—such as internally reporting the number of Patriot Express loans made each quarter and deciding not to renew a top lender's delegated authority to make Patriot Express loans based on ongoing monitoring, as previously mentioned—but these activities are not the same as program evaluation.[51] Because there are many more 7(a) loans, which therefore pose a greater risk to SBA than the smaller volume of Patriot Express loans, SBA officials told us that they have focused more resources on evaluating the performance of 7(a) loans.

In addition to Patriot Express, SBA has authorized other pilot loan programs that it has subsequently not evaluated when making decisions about the future of the program. For example, in 2010, SBA's OIG conducted an assessment of the Community Express program, which was established in 1999, to determine, among other things, whether the program was properly structured to ensure success and minimize the risk of fraud.[52] This assessment was completed in response to a concern presented by SBA to the SBA OIG regarding poor performance of the Community Express program. In this assessment, the SBA OIG found that SBA did not establish measurable performance goals and outcomes for evaluating the Community Express program until 9 years after the pilot's inception. Further, though the OIG determined that these performance measures were adequate, SBA had extended the pilot without using the measures to assess the program's effectiveness.[53] Similarly, in 2006 the OIG found that SBA had not reviewed the SBA Express program—which was initiated in 1995 as a pilot—to determine, among other things, if final rules and regulations would be developed.[54]

---

[51]On July 23, 2013, SBA provided us documentation on some calculations of performance (as of Jan. 31, 2009) of Patriot Express loans originated from July 2007 through January 2009.

[52]SBA, Office of Inspector General, *Assessment of the Community Express Pilot Loan Program*, Report No. 10-12 (Washington, D.C.: Aug. 25, 2010). The Community Express program authorized approved lenders to adopt streamlined and expedited loan procedures to provide financial and technical assistance to borrowers in the nation's underserved communities.

[53]SBA terminated the Community Express program on April 30, 2011.

[54]SBA, Office of Inspector General, *Management Advisory Report: Policies and Procedures for the SBA Express and Community Express Loan Programs*, Report No. 6-34 (Washington, D.C.: Sept. 29, 2006).

Rather than evaluate the program to develop regulations, SBA continued to extend the program as a pilot for 9 years until Congress made it permanent in 2004. Because of this lack of review and establishment of regulations, the OIG recommended in 2006 that the agency issue regulations to, among other things, ensure that that SBA has legally enforceable rules to manage the program. SBA agreed that regulations were needed for the program, but did not establish such regulations, according to OIG officials.

The Administrator of SBA has the authority to suspend, modify, or waive rules for a limited period of time to test new programs or ideas through pilot programs, but this authorization does not include a specific requirement for SBA to conduct a pilot evaluation.[55] Congress has established an annual limit for the number of loans made through pilots within the 7(a) program. Specifically, no more than 10 percent of all 7(a) loans guaranteed in a fiscal year can be made through a pilot program.[56] According to SBA officials, a pilot program's duration and the number of times the agency can extend it depend on the length of time needed to complete testing of the pilot. However, as shown by SBA's experience with the Patriot Express, Community Express, and SBA Express pilots, SBA does not always test pilots or evaluate their effects when initiating pilot programs under its own authority.

Without designing and conducting evaluations of the pilot programs it conducts under its own authority, SBA has little information to assess the performance of the programs and their effects on eligible borrowers, which could be used in decisions on the future of these pilots, including the Patriot Express program. For example, information on the financial performance of veteran-owned businesses participating in various SBA loan programs could help inform policy decisions. Further, the information drawn from an evaluation of Patriot Express could also be used to inform training and counseling resources for veterans. In turn, input from veteran borrowers participating in SBA loan programs and from counselors at SBA resource partners assisting veteran borrowers could provide a basis for improvements in existing SBA loan programs.

---

[55]13 C.F.R. § 120.3.

[56]15 U.S.C. § 636(a)(25).

SBA's Internal Controls May Not Provide Assurance of Borrower Eligibility

SBA has two primary internal control activities to ensure lender compliance with borrower eligibility requirements—on-site examinations and purchase reviews. However, these reviews may not provide the agency with reasonable assurance that Patriot Express loans are only made to eligible borrowers. SBA only reviews a small number of Patriot Express loans for eligibility as part of on-site examinations, and although it examines eligibility as part of purchase reviews, these reviews occur only for loans that have defaulted, in some cases long after an ineligible borrower may have received proceeds from a Patriot Express loan. In addition, although SBA officials told us that they expect borrowers to maintain their eligibility throughout the term of the loan, SBA has not developed procedures to provide reasonable assurance that Patriot Express loans continue to serve eligible borrowers after a loan is disbursed. Internal control standards for federal agencies and GAO's fraud-prevention framework state that oversight programs should be designed to ensure that ongoing monitoring occurs in the course of normal operations.[57] Furthermore, the intent of the Patriot Express program is to support eligible members of the military community. Without greater review of Patriot Express transactions during on-site examinations of lenders and requirements for lenders to ensure that borrowers remain eligible after disbursement, there is an increased risk that the proceeds of Patriot Express loans will be provided to or used by borrowers who do not qualify for the program.

SBA Has Reviewed Few Patriot Express Loans during On-Site Examinations of the Largest Participating Lenders

GAO's fraud-prevention framework identifies three elements needed to minimize fraud: (1) up-front preventive controls, (2) detection and monitoring, and (3) investigations and prosecutions.[58] For Patriot Express, SBA addresses the first element of the framework through the steps lenders are required to take under their delegated authority to ensure borrower eligibility at loan origination. It addresses the third element by the steps it must take to refer potential cases of fraud to its OIG for investigation and possible prosecution. However, we found that SBA's detection and monitoring—the second element of the framework—

---

[57]See GAO, *Standards for Internal Control in the Federal Government*, GAO/AIMD-00-21.3.1 (Washington, D.C.: November 1999) and *Service-Disabled Veteran-Owned Small Business Program: Fraud Prevention Controls Needed to Improve Program Integrity*, GAO-10-740T (Washington, D.C.: May 24, 2010).

[58]GAO-10-740T.

could be strengthened. One of SBA's primary monitoring activities to provide reasonable assurance that Patriot Express loans are made only to eligible borrowers is the reviews it performs as part of its on-site examinations of lenders. However, since the program's inception in 2007, SBA has reviewed only a small number of Patriot Express loans for the 10 largest Patriot Express lenders.[59]

SBA does not conduct specific Patriot Express program examinations. Instead, it reviews a lender's compliance with Patriot Express program eligibility requirements as part of its examination of the lender's 7(a) program or as part of a safety and soundness examination of an SBLC.[60] These examinations are known as risk-based reviews or safety and soundness examinations for SBLCs.[61] During these reviews, SBA draws a sample of loans from a lender's files to assess, among other things, whether the loans met specific program eligibility requirements at the time of approval.[62] For example, if an SBA examiner selects a Patriot Express loan, the examiner is expected to review the lender's documents to determine whether that loan was provided to a veteran or other eligible member of the military community. The lenders must document in their files how they determined the borrower's eligibility for the Patriot Express program, including what Department of Defense and Department of Veteran Affairs documents they used to verify veteran status. Additionally, the examiner is expected to review lender documentation to determine whether the veteran or other eligible borrower owned 51 percent or more of the small business at the time of loan approval. As part of the risk-based review, SBA's examiners are required to compile a list of all eligibility deficiencies by issue type and errors, and identify any trends of deficiencies that warrant lender attention.

---

[59]These are the top 10 lenders based on the number of Patriot Express loans made since the program's inception.

[60]In this context, 7(a) refers to (1) regular (nondelegated) 7(a) loans, (2) delegated 7(a) loans made by PLP lenders, and (3) all subprograms including Patriot Express and SBA Express.

[61]The risk-based review and examination process allocates on-site review resources to SBA lenders with higher-risk characteristics in terms of credit risk, portfolio performance, SBA exposure, and compliance.

[62]Based on our review of examinations of the 10 largest Patriot Express lenders, SBA selected the sample of loans based on (1) a random sample of the lender's SBA loans and (2) a judgmental sample to ensure that loans from different SBA programs (e.g., 7(a), SBA Express, Patriot Express) were selected.

We reviewed the most recent 7(a) risk-based examination and an SBLC safety and soundness examination for the 10 largest Patriot Express lenders and found that with the exception of 3 lenders, SBA examined few Patriot Express loans. As table 4 shows, for the first 3 lenders, SBA sampled at least six Patriot Express loans during the examination. However, for the remaining lenders, SBA sampled one or two loans at two of the lenders and did not sample any Patriot Express loans at the other 5 lenders. For the 5 lenders in table 4 for which SBA sampled at least one Patriot Express loan, 4 lenders were found by SBA to be in compliance with eligibility requirements. For the remaining lender, SBA did not report on its assessment of eligibility requirements in the examination.

Table 4: Patriot Express Loans Sampled in Most Recent SBA Examination and Number of Patriot Express Loans Made by Top 10 Lenders from 2007 to the Year Prior to Examination

Lender	Year of most recent examinations	Patriot Express loans sampled	Number of Patriot Express loans made from 2007 to year prior to examination
Lender 1	2010	35	1,285
Lender 2	2012	8	172
Lender 3	2010	6	223
Lender 4	2012	2	410
Lender 5	2012	1	99
Lender 6	2012	0	220
Lender 7	2011	0	170
Lender 8	2012	0	148
Lender 9	2011	0	140
Lender 10	2012	0	68

Source: GAO analysis of SBA data.

SBA officials said SBA examined few or no Patriot Express loans for 7 of these 10 lenders because Patriot Express comprised a small percentage of these lenders' overall lending. At six of the 7 lenders, the Patriot Express loan volume as of the program's inception to the year prior to the examination ranged from 1 percent to 8 percent of their overall SBA lending activities.[63] However, while these percentages are relatively small, in a program that has a specific target population—veterans and other eligible members of the military community—assessing lenders' compliance with eligibility requirements is particularly important to help ensure that the guaranteed loans are assisting only eligible veteran entrepreneurs as intended. The monitoring of borrower eligibility that occurs through on-site examinations is a key internal control and fraud-prevention element for Patriot Express because the loan program serves a specific population with loan provisions intended only for this population of borrowers.[64]

Another primary internal control that SBA uses to monitor borrower eligibility is the purchase reviews that it conducts for loans that have defaulted and for which the lender is seeking the guarantee payment.[65] As part of the purchase review, an SBA official must review documentation relied upon by the lender to determine whether the borrower was eligible for the program. However, purchase reviews are only conducted for loans that have defaulted and would not identify ineligible borrowers who continue to make their loan payments. Additionally, ineligible borrowers may have the loan for years before ultimately defaulting. Because SBA conducts so few on-site examinations of Patriot Express loans, opportunities to identify these ineligible borrowers prior to a default are limited. For a program with a specific target population, an increased emphasis on reviewing borrower eligibility is important. Without sampling more Patriot Express loans during examinations, SBA may have difficulty identifying deficiencies related to eligibility. This, in turn, could increase the risk to SBA of Patriot Express loans being provided to borrowers who do not qualify for the program.

---

[63]For the other lender, Patriot Express loan volume as of the date of the examination was 45 percent of their overall SBA lending activities.

[64]Regular (nondelegated) 7(a) loans, delegated 7(a) loans made by PLP lenders, and SBA Express loans do not have any comparable specific targeted borrowers, other than the common goal of serving small businesses.

[65]More broadly, the purchase review is SBA's primary control for ensuring lender compliance and preventing improper payments.

SBA Has Not Provided Clarity to Lenders Regarding Borrowers' Ongoing Ownership Requirements

Although SBA requires lenders to assess borrowers' eligibility for Patriot Express at the time of loan approval, it does not require them to reassess eligibility, including the 51 percent ownership requirement, after the loan has been disbursed. SBA does not have a stated requirement for borrowers to maintain their eligibility after the loan has been disbursed, but SBA officials told us that they do expect borrowers to maintain 51 percent ownership after a loan has been disbursed to remain eligible for the program. SBA requires that borrowers certify that they will not change the ownership structure or sell the business without the consent of the lender.[66] Additionally, SBA officials told us that in the event of a borrower default, a lender could lose the SBA guarantee if the borrower had sold his or her business to an individual who does not qualify for a Patriot Express loan. However, in the examples below, lenders may not be aware of changes in ownership structure or sale of the business if the borrower has not informed lenders of such actions and the lender is not periodically reassessing Patriot Express eligibility after the loan has been disbursed. Borrowers may initially be approved as meeting Patriot Express eligibility requirements at the time of loan approval, but subsequent events may affect their eligibility and result in the loan being used by an ineligible borrower. For example, according to SBA OIG officials, a business may recruit a veteran to pose as the majority business owner in order to be eligible for a Patriot Express loan and add the veteran to legal ownership documents that would be provided to the lender when applying for the loan. Once the loan is disbursed, however, the business could reduce the ownership interest or remove the veteran as an owner of the business. Such cases could also involve the businesses giving the veteran a kickback after the loan was disbursed. In another example, after the loan has been disbursed, an eligible Patriot Express borrower might sell all or part of his or her ownership interest in the qualifying business. In these examples, an ineligible party benefits from the Patriot Express loan proceeds.

These examples illustrate the importance of effective monitoring and detection activities, which are key internal controls and an element of the fraud-prevention framework. Detection and monitoring controls include activities such as periodically evaluating lender procedures to provide

---

[66]Borrowers who own at least 51 percent of the business must personally guarantee all loans, including Patriot Express loans. In order for borrowers to be released from this guarantee, such as through the sale of their ownership interest in the business, lenders must obtain SBA's approval.

reasonable assurance that only eligible borrowers obtain loans and benefit from the program as intended. Such assurance is particularly important in a program that has specific eligibility requirements and was created to serve a specific population. Four of six lenders we spoke with thought that borrowers needed to remain eligible for the loan after disbursement, but these four lenders stated that they did not think that they needed to check on borrowers to make sure that they remain eligible after loan disbursement. The other two lenders we spoke with told us that they did not think ongoing borrower eligibility was a requirement of the program. In the absence of formal SBA eligibility procedures to ensure that only borrowers who maintain 51 percent ownership receive assistance after a loan has been disbursed, Patriot Express loan proceeds may ultimately be used by those other than the intended program beneficiaries. As a result, SBA may not have reasonable assurance that Patriot Express loans are serving the intended population.

Conclusions

Prior to 2007, SBA served the small business needs of veteran entrepreneurs through its 7(a) and SBA Express programs. SBA established the Patriot Express Pilot Loan initiative in 2007 as a targeted effort to provide veterans and other eligible members of the military community access to capital to establish or expand small businesses. However, the effect this initiative has had on the small business financing needs of veterans and other entrepreneurs in the military community is unknown. While SBA recently announced an initiative to increase overall lending to veteran small businesses by $475 million over the next 5 years, the role of the Patriot Express pilot initiative is unclear given that SBA has yet to evaluate the effectiveness of the program. Based on our analysis, with the exception of 2007, Patriot Express loans made to veterans have had a relatively high default rate, and losses for the initiative have exceeded its income. Moreover, SBA has not conducted an evaluation of the pilot initiative that would include standards for pilot performance, comparative measures with other programs that may also serve veterans, methods for data collection, evaluation of data on the performance of the loans, data and analysis from external reports and evaluations, and time frames for completion. Although SBA officials said that they have begun to hold meetings on what information they will need to assess the performance of Patriot Express loans, SBA has not established a plan to evaluate the program, and only a few months remain before the current extension of the program is set to end. Program evaluations can be useful in informing future program decisions, including SBA's planned efforts to expand lending to veterans.

In addition, the lack of an evaluation or an evaluation plan for Patriot Express follows a pattern for SBA pilot loan programs. As with the Patriot Express pilot initiative, SBA has authorized other pilot loan programs in the past that it has subsequently not evaluated when making decisions about the future of those programs. SBA's past experience with pilots raises questions about its commitment and capacity to fully implement pilots that include a rigorous evaluation. Without evaluations of pilot initiatives, SBA lacks the information needed to determine if a pilot program is achieving its intended goals and whether it should be cancelled, modified, or expanded.

Finally, SBA's reliance on lenders to assess borrowers' eligibility for Patriot Express highlights the importance of strong internal controls over lenders to ensure that only eligible borrowers are served by the program. Federal internal control guidance and GAO's fraud-prevention framework indicate that program controls should include monitoring and detection. However, SBA currently samples few Patriot Express loans during on-site examinations. In addition, while SBA expects borrowers to maintain 51 percent ownership after a loan has been disbursed, SBA has not developed procedures to require lenders to verify that the 51 percent ownership requirement is maintained, nor does it monitor the lenders' activities to ensure eligibility after disbursement. As a result, SBA's internal controls may not provide the necessary assurance that Patriot Express loans are made to and used by only eligible members of the military community—the intended mission of the program.

Recommendations for Executive Action

As SBA considers whether or not to extend the Patriot Express Pilot Loan program, we recommend that the Administrator of SBA design and implement an evaluation plan for the pilot program that assesses how well the Patriot Express pilot is achieving program goals and objectives regarding its performance and its effect on eligible borrowers. The evaluation plan should include information such as

- evaluation of SBA data on performance of Patriot Express loans;

- evaluation of borrowers served by Patriot Express in relation to veteran borrowers served by other SBA loan programs; and

- review of relevant SBA OIG reports and other external studies.

To help ensure that SBA makes informed decisions on the future of pilot programs it creates under its own authority, we recommend that the Administrator of SBA require the agency to design an evaluation plan for any such pilot program prior to implementation—including an assessment of the program's performance and its effect on program recipients—and to consider the results of such an evaluation before any pilot is extended.

To help ensure that Patriot Express loans are only provided to members of the military community eligible to participate in the program, we recommend that the Administrator of SBA strengthen existing internal controls, including

- sampling a larger number of Patriot Express loans during examinations;

- developing a requirement in SBA's Standard Operating Procedures for lenders to verify the eligibility of the borrower, including the 51 percent ownership requirement, after the loan has been disbursed; and

- periodically monitoring the lenders' implementation of this eligibility requirement.

Agency Comments

We provided the Administrator of the Small Business Administration with a draft of this report for review and comment. On August 26, 2013, the SBA liaison—Program Manager, Office of Congressional and Legislative Affairs—provided us with the following comment via email on the draft. He stated that the agency will consider the findings from this report as it reviews the extension of the Patriot Express Pilot Loan Program. SBA also provided technical comments, which we incorporated into the report where appropriate.

We are sending copies of this report to SBA, appropriate congressional committees and members, and other interested parties. The report also is available at no charge on the GAO website at http://www.gao.gov.

If you or your staff have any questions about this report, please contact me at (202) 512-8678 or shearw@gao.gov. Contact points for our Offices of Congressional Relations and Public Affairs may be found on the last page of this report. GAO staff who made major contributions to this report are listed in appendix III.

William B. Shear
Director, Financial Markets and
    Community Investment

Appendix I: Objectives, Scope, and Methodology

Our objectives were to examine (1) trends in the Patriot Express program and related Small Business Administration (SBA) guarantee programs, including performance of these loans, and what is known about the costs of the Patriot Express program, (2) the benefits and challenges of the Patriot Express program for members of the military community eligible to participate as well as training and counseling opportunities available to them, and (3) what internal controls SBA has in place to ensure that the Patriot Express program is available only to eligible members of the military community.

To describe trends in the Patriot Express program, including how Patriot Express loans approved from 2007 through 2012 have performed, we obtained SBA loan-level data on loans approved from the second quarter of 2007 through the fourth quarter of 2012 for Patriot Express and from the first quarter of 2007 through the fourth quarter of 2012 for the 7(a), and SBA Express programs. We took a number of steps to develop a dataset we could use for our analyses.[1] We excluded loans with missing disbursement dates unless they had positive balances at some point in their history, which to us indicated loan activity. Additionally, we excluded loans that in December 2012 were indicated to have been cancelled. Once we arrived at our final dataset, we analyzed it for various performance measures, including default rates.[2] A loan was defined as defaulted (purchased) if it had a purchase date on or after the approval date. Specifically, we analyzed the default rates by the following categories:

- *Cohort analysis*—Using the loan approval date data field, we identified loans for all three programs and grouped them in calendar year cohorts reflecting loans approved from 2007 through 2012. Once these loans were identified, we calculated the default rates, total number of loans, and total loan values approved from 2007 through 2012 for all three programs.

---

[1]Because SBA provided us with loans from Patriot Express, 7(a), and SBA Express in one file, we used the subprogram code field to identify loans from the different programs. In the process of inquiring with SBA about SBA Express loans, SBA identified 55 loans that according to the subprogram code were SBA Express loans but that SBA, through the use of another field we did not have access to, identified as Export Express loans.

[2]In this report, we define default rate as the number of loans that SBA has purchased from the lender divided by the outstanding number of loans approved.

- *Loan amount*—Using the gross amount approved data field, we
  identified the number of loans by loan amounts that were approved for
  all three programs from 2007 through 2012. We grouped these loans
  into major categories based on requirements of the programs. For
  example, we focused on loans below $25,000 because the Patriot
  Express and SBA Express programs require no collateral for these
  loans. We selected the next category, loans valued between $25,001
  and $150,000, based on the guarantee percentage change from 85
  percent to 75 percent for Patriot Express and 7(a) that occurs at
  $150,000. We selected the next two categories of loans valued
  between $150,001 and $350,000 and between $350,001 and
  $500,000 to capture the maximum allowable loans for SBA Express
  and Patriot Express, respectively. Additionally, we focused on loans
  valued between $500,001 and $1,000,000 and between $1,000,001 to
  $5,000,000 to account for the larger loan amounts for 7(a). Once
  these loans were identified by loan amounts, we calculated the default
  rates for all three programs based on loans approved from 2007
  through 2012.

- *Lender concentration*—Using the main bank data field, we identified
  the top 11 lenders based on the number of approved Patriot Express
  loans from 2007 through 2012. Once these lenders were identified,
  we calculated the default rates, average loan amounts, and total loan
  amounts approved from 2007 through 2012. Additionally, we
  calculated the relative percentage of loans made by each of the top
  11 lenders compared to the overall number of Patriot Express loans
  approved from 2007 through 2012. After we identified that one lender
  accounted for 26 percent of all Patriot Express loans approved, we
  calculated the relative percentage and default rates of this one lender
  compared to all other lenders from 2007 through 2012.

- *Veteran status*—Using a data field that identifies borrowers based on
  their veteran status, we identified borrowers that self-identified as
  either a veteran, service-disabled veteran, or Vietnam-era veteran
  from each of the three programs. Once these loans were identified,
  we calculated the default rates, total number of loans, and total loan
  values approved from 2001 through 2012 for SBA Express and 7(a),
  and 2007 through 2012 for Patriot Express.

- *New Business*—Using the new or existing business data field and
  information provided by SBA, we identified new businesses that had
  been in operation 2 years or less prior to loan approval, and existing
  businesses that had been in operation for more than 2 years at time of
  loan approval. Once these loans were identified, we calculated the

relative percentage of new businesses for loans approved from 2007
through 2012.

- *Use of Proceeds*—Using the loan proceeds data field and information
  provided by SBA, we identified the most common use of loan
  proceeds for Patriot Express loans approved from 2007 through 2012.

- *Small Business Portfolio Scores (SBPS)*—Using a data field that
  identifies borrowers by their SBPS scores, based on available data,
  we grouped businesses based on having a low (139 or lower),
  medium (140-179) or high (180 or greater) SBPS score. We then
  calculated the default rates, total number of loans, total value of loans,
  and relative percentage of loans for Patriot Express, SBA Express
  and 7(a).

For all of our analyses on the performance of Patriot Express, 7(a), and
SBA Express loans, we did not weight default rates by loan amount. In
addition, for each analysis we did not include loans with missing values.
To assess data reliability, we interviewed SBA representatives from the
Office of Performance and Systems Management and the Office of Credit
Risk Management about how they collected data and helped ensure data
integrity. We also reviewed internal agency procedures for ensuring data
reliability. In addition, we conducted reasonableness checks on the data
to identify any missing, erroneous, or outlying figures, and when
necessary, submitted follow-up questions to SBA officials at the Office of
Performance and Systems Management and the Office of Credit Risk
Management to clarify our understanding of the data. Through our
electronic data testing, we identified irregularities in the data in a small
percentage of cases, such as loans with approval amounts in excess of
what we understood to be the limits of the program or loans with disbursal
dates, but zero dollars disbursed. However, SBA was able to explain
these cases as being due to periods in which the limits of the program
were temporarily expanded, or provided other explanations. We did not
find more than a minimal amount of missing values in fields relating to
approved amount, approval year of purchase, and key variables for our
analysis of performance. As such, we determined that the data were
sufficiently reliable for our purposes.

To describe what is known about the costs of the Patriot Express program
from 2007 through 2012, we obtained and analyzed SBA cash-flow data
on SBA purchases of defaulted loans, as well as data on offsets, which
include the following three categories: (1) upfront fees generated by the
program at time of approval, (2) annual fees based on loans in a lender's
portfolio in good standing, and (3) recoveries either from the proceeds of

attached collateral to the defaulted loans or subsequent payments on loans following purchase by SBA. Additionally, we reviewed SBA guidance, the agency's standard operating procedures, and inspector general reports to obtain more information on cash-flow data. To assess data reliability, we interviewed SBA representatives from the Office of Financial Analysis and Modeling, the Office of Performance and Systems Management, and the Office of Credit Risk Management to understand how they collect data and help ensure the integrity of the cash-flow data, as well as how they use these data for budgetary purposes. We also submitted follow-up questions to SBA officials at both the Office of Financial Analysis and Modeling and the Office of Credit Risk Management to clarify our understanding of the data. We determined that the data were sufficiently reliable for our purposes.

To assess the effect of the Patriot Express program on members of the military community eligible to participate in the program, we conducted semi-structured interviews with a sample of 24 Patriot Express loan recipients about how the Patriot Express loan affected their businesses and their views on how the program could be improved.[3] We selected this nongeneralizable, stratified random sample of loan recipients to reflect two factors: the recipient's loan amount and the number of Patriot Express loans their lender has made since the program's inception to 2012. While the results of these interviews could not be generalized to all Patriot Express loan recipients, they provided insight into the benefits and challenges of the program.[4] Table 5 below highlights selected characteristics of the Patriot Express loan recipients we interviewed.[5]

---

[3]In order to arrive at our final sample of 24 Patriot Express loan recipients, we contacted or attempted to contact 132 Patriot Express loan recipients. We found that a high percentage of SBA's contact information on these borrowers was inaccurate or missing. SBA officials told us that they do not contact borrowers but that if they needed to and found that the borrower's contact information was inaccurate or missing in SBA's data, they could get the correct contact information from the lender.

[4]For loan recipients that we contacted who received multiple Patriot Express loans, we only analyzed the experiences drawn from the Patriot Express loan included in our sample.

[5]All 24 loan recipients we met with were still in business at the time we interviewed them. In contacting Patriot Express loan recipients, we encountered some borrowers who had gone out of business or declared bankruptcy, and they declined to speak with us.

Table 5: Selected Characteristics of Loan Recipients Included in Our Sample

Characteristic	Number of loan recipients in sample[a]
Patriot Express loan amount	
Less than $20,000	9
$20,000-$149,999	10
Greater than $150,000	5
Lender	
Top 11 Patriot Express lenders[b]	13
Remainder of lenders	11
Loan approval year	
2008	3
2009	8
2010	4
2011	5
2012	4
Type of eligible borrower	
Veteran	19
Spouse	5
Type of loan product	
Term loan	18
Line of credit	6

Source: GAO analysis of SBA data.

[a]The number of loan recipients within each characteristic category total to 24 and individual loan recipients are categorized into multiple categories.

[b]These are the top 11 lenders that made the most number of Patriot Express loans from 2007 through 2012.

To obtain the perspectives of veteran entrepreneurs who were aware of the Patriot Express program and appeared to meet the eligibility requirements for a Patriot Express loan but instead obtained an SBA Express or 7(a) loan, we attempted to contact a nongeneralizable sample of veterans who participated in these two other programs.[6] Of the 15 SBA Express veteran loan recipients and 16 7(a) veteran loan recipients whom we were able to contact, we interviewed 4 veteran entrepreneurs who obtained a 7(a) loan.[7] We conducted interviews with these recipients to inquire about their experiences with the 7(a) loan and to obtain their views on the Patriot Express program.

We also interviewed a sample of lenders to obtain their perspectives on the benefits and challenges of the Patriot Express program. We selected the top 10 lenders that made the greatest number of Patriot Express loans from 2007 through 2012.[8] The selected lenders made approximately 48 percent of the Patriot Express loans over this period and consisted of various types of lending institutions, including large banks, a credit union, and a small business lending company (SBLC).[9] While the results of these interviews could not be generalized to all lenders participating in the Patriot Express program, they provided insight into the key differences in administering the program as compared to other SBA loan programs. To obtain a broader set of lender perspectives on the program, we interviewed representatives from the National Association of Government Guaranteed Lenders (NAGGL), a trade organization representing SBA 7(a) lenders. We also interviewed representatives from three veteran service organizations with an interest in veteran entrepreneurship, namely the Veteran Entrepreneurship Task (VET) Force, Veteran Chamber of Commerce, and American Legion, to gather information on the benefits and challenges of the program that their members have experienced. Finally, we interviewed SBA officials from the Offices of Capital Access and Veterans Business Development

---

[6]To sample veteran entrepreneurs who appeared to meet the eligibility requirements for a Patriot Express loan, we limited our sample to veterans who received SBA Express and 7(a) loans that were $500,000 or less (the same loan amount range as Patriot Express) and made after June 2007, when the Patriot Express program was initiated. Information on veteran status for SBA Express and 7(a) loan recipients is self-reported by the borrower and is not verified by the lender. Therefore, this information may not accurately or consistently capture all veterans who have received a loan through these programs.

[7]As part of our attempt to contact these veterans, we found that some were not aware of the Patriot Express program. Because we wanted to obtain perspectives of veteran entrepreneurs that received other SBA loans and could share their views on Patriot Express, we did not interview those that were unaware of the program.

[8]Two of the top 10 lenders we contacted declined to speak to us.

[9]The term "large bank" refers to banks with over $10 billion in assets.

who are responsible for managing and promoting the program. We
interviewed these officials to obtain their perspectives on identified
benefits and challenges to the program, promotion of the program and its
lenders, and efforts to evaluate the program's effect on members of the
military community eligible to participate.

To describe other ways in which veteran entrepreneurs accessed capital,
as part of our interviews with Patriot Express and 7(a) loan recipients, as
well as selected lenders and veteran service organizations, we also
inquired about other ways in which veterans can gain access to capital.
To describe the training and counseling efforts SBA has in place for
veteran entrepreneurs, we obtained and reviewed reports by the
Interagency Task Force on Veterans Small Business Development from
2011 and 2012.[10] We also reviewed SBA documents related to training
and counseling resources and SBA information on the number of
veterans that have used these resources from 2008 through 2012. We
also interviewed SBA officials responsible for these efforts. To describe
the perspectives of veteran entrepreneurs on the effectiveness of SBA's
training and counseling efforts, we reviewed results from SBA's annual
Veteran Business Outreach Center client satisfaction survey from 2008
through 2012. We also interviewed the selected veteran service
organizations and Patriot Express and 7(a) loan recipients on their
perspective on the quality of training and counseling efforts sponsored by
SBA.

To determine SBA's prior experience with pilots initiated under its own
authority, we obtained and reviewed pertinent regulations on SBA's
authority to initiate pilots and applicable limitations. We also reviewed two
SBA Office of Inspector General (OIG) reports pertaining to SBA's
experience with the Community Express and SBA Express pilot

---

[10]The Interagency Task Force on Veterans Small Business Development was created in
2010 by the President and is chaired by the Administrator of SBA. It is tasked to, among
other things, develop proposals related to improving access to capital for veteran-owned
businesses and increasing training and counseling services provided to veteran
entrepreneurs. For the task force's annual reports, see Interagency Task Force on
Veterans Small Business Development, *Report to the President: Empowering Veterans
Through Entrepreneurship*, (Washington D.C.: Nov. 1, 2011) and Interagency Task Force
on Veterans Small Business Development, *Heroes on the Home Front: Supporting
Veteran Success as Small Business Owners* (Washington D.C.: Nov. 29, 2012).

programs.[11] To assess how well SBA has conducted pilot programs, including Patriot Express, we reviewed components identified in our previous work as key features of a program evaluation and an evaluation plan.[12]

To evaluate SBA's internal controls related to ensuring that the Patriot Express program is available only to members of the military community eligible to participate in the program, we reviewed SBA's standard operating procedures related to borrower eligibility requirements. Also, as part of our interviews with the selected lenders and borrowers previously discussed, we inquired about the documentation used to establish eligibility for the program. To determine how SBA oversees lenders to ensure they are complying with the Patriot Express eligibility requirements, we reviewed SBA's standard operating procedures related to lender oversight. We also obtained copies of examination reports for the top 10 Patriot Express lenders (based on the number of loans made) from 2007 through 2012. We reviewed these reports to determine the number of Patriot Express loans sampled during the examination and SBA's disposition on whether the lender was complying with SBA rules and regulations related to borrower eligibility. Additionally, we interviewed officials from the Office of Credit Risk Management to inquire about SBA's oversight of its lenders as it relates to the Patriot Express program. To determine how SBA reviews defaulted loans as part of its purchase review, we reviewed SBA's standard operating procedures related to these reviews, as well as an SBA OIG report on improper payments, which also described the purchase reviews.[13] We also met with officials from SBA's Office of Financial Program Operations to understand how SBA staff review submissions from lenders requesting that SBA purchase defaulted loans. Finally, to help assess the extent to which the Patriot Express program could be susceptible to fraud and abuse, we reviewed

---

[11]SBA, Office of Inspector General, *Assessment of the Community Express Pilot Loan Program*, Report No. 10-12 (Washington, D.C.: Aug. 25, 2010) and SBA, Office of Inspector General, *Management Advisory Report: Policies and Procedures for the SBA Express and Community Express Loan Programs*, Report No. 6-34 (Washington, D.C.: Sept. 29, 2006).

[12]GAO-13-519SP, GAO-13-570, and GAO, *Designing Evaluations: 2012 Revision*, GAO-12-208G (Washington D.C.: January 2012).

[13]SBA, Office of Inspector General, *The Small Business Administration's Improper Payment Rate for 7(a) Guaranty Purchases Remains Significantly Underestimated*, Report No. 13-07 (Washington, D.C.: Nov. 15, 2012).

SBA's internal control standards related to ensuring that Patriot Express loans were made to eligible members of the military community. We compared these internal controls to federal internal control standards, as well as to GAO's Fraud Prevention Framework.[14] We also interviewed officials from SBA's Office of Inspector General to learn about scenarios under which the Patriot Express program could be susceptible to fraud and abuse.

We conducted this performance audit from November 2012 to September 2013 in accordance with generally accepted government auditing standards. Those standards require that we plan and perform the audit to obtain sufficient, appropriate evidence to provide a reasonable basis for our findings and conclusions based on our audit objectives. We believe that the evidence obtained provides a reasonable basis for our findings and conclusions based on our audit objectives.

---

[14]See GAO, *Standards for Internal Control in the Federal Government*, GAO/AIMD-00-21.3.1 (Washington, D.C.: November 1999) and GAO, *Service-Disabled Veteran-Owned Small Business Program: Fraud Prevention Controls Needed to Improve Program Integrity,* GAO-10-740T (Washington, D.C.: May 24, 2010).

Appendix II: Comparison of SBA's 7(a), SBA Express, and Patriot Express Loan Programs

In addition to the Patriot Express pilot program, there are several delivery methods within the SBA 7(a) program, including regular (nondelegated) 7(a), delegated 7(a) loans made by lenders in the Preferred Lenders Program (PLP), and SBA Express loans.[1] While all delivery methods provide a borrower with an SBA-guaranteed loan, there are several similarities and differences between these three programs, such as eligibility restrictions, maximum loan amounts, and percent of guarantee. Table 6 below compares the key features of these three loan programs discussed throughout this report.

Table 6: Comparison of 7(a), SBA Express, and Patriot Express Loan Programs

	7(a)	SBA Express	Patriot Express
Type of loan	Short-term (12 months) or long-term loan. No revolving features.	Same as 7(a) or may be used for revolving lines of credit (up to 7 years).	Same as SBA Express.
Use of loan proceeds	SBA-guaranteed loan proceeds may be used for the following purposes:[a] 1. Acquisition of land or purchase, construction or renovation of buildings 2. Improvement of a site 3. Acquisition and installation of fixed assets 4. Inventory 5. Supplies 6. Raw Materials 7. Working Capital 8. Refinancing	Same as 7(a) plus Renewable Energy and Energy Efficiency Loans.	Same as 7(a).
Loan decision process	Regular (nondelegated) 7(a) loans: SBA approves the loan for both credit and eligibility. Delegated 7(a) loans made by PLP lenders: Lender is delegated the credit decision and completes a checklist for eligibility which SBA reviews.	Authorized lenders make loan approval decisions, including credit determinations, without prior SBA review.	Same as SBA Express.
Target processing time	Regular (nondelegated) 7(a) loans: 6 business days Delegated 7(a) loans made by PLP lenders: 1 business day	1 business day.	Same as SBA Express.

[1]As mentioned previously, when we refer to 7(a) loans, we are referring to (1) regular (nondelegated) 7(a) loans and (2) delegated 7(a) loans made by PLP lenders, unless otherwise noted.

	7(a)	SBA Express	Patriot Express

Eligibility restrictions	1. The small business applicant must:[b]
	  a. Be an operating business
	  b. Be organized for profit
	  c. Be located in the U.S.
	  d. Be small (as defined by 13 C.F.R. 121)
	  e. Demonstrate a need for the desired credit
	2. Lender must certify that credit is not available elsewhere on reasonable terms.[c]
	3. Applicant must show that funds are not available from alternative sources, including personal resources of the principals.[d]
	4. The business must be an eligible type of business.[e]
		Same as 7(a).	Same as 7(a).
			
			In addition to meeting the eligibility requirements of the 7(a) program, the business must be 51% or more owned and controlled by one or more of the following:
			• Veteran, certain active-duty military, reservist or National Guard member
			• A spouse of any of the above groups, or
			• A widowed spouse of a service member or veteran who died during service, or of a service-connected disability.

Maximum loan amount[f]	$5,000,000	$350,000	$500,000
Percent of guarantee	• 85% for loans $150,000 or less. • 75% for loans over $150,000.	50%	Same as 7(a).
Collateral policy	Available collateral (liquidation value) up to loan amount.	No collateral is required for loans $25,000 or less. Lenders may use their own collateral policies used for their non-SBA-guaranteed loans for loans more than $25,000.	• Same as SBA Express for loans $350,000 or less. • Same as 7(a) for loans more than $350,000.
SBA guarantee fees	**Lender's Annual Ongoing Fee:**[g] Not to exceed 0.55% of the outstanding balance of the guaranteed portion of loan **Lender Guarantee Fee:**[h] <u>Loans with maturities of 12 months or less:</u> 0.25% of the guaranteed portion <u>Loans with maturities of over 12 months:</u> • $150,000 or less: 2% of the guaranteed portion • $150,001 - $700,000: 3% of the guaranteed portion • $700,001 - $5,000,000: 3.5% of the guaranteed portion up to $1,000,000 plus 3.75% of the guaranteed portion over $1 million	Same as 7(a).	Same as 7(a).

	7(a)	SBA Express	Patriot Express

Borrower Packaging and Other Services Fees[i]	• Packaging and other service fees that a lender charges a borrower based on a percentage of the loan amount cannot exceed:
	
	  • 3% for loans $50,000 or less
	
	  • 2% for loans between $50,001 to $1 million and an additional 0.25% on the remaining amount over $1 million (maximum fee of $30,000).
		Same as 7(a).	Same as 7(a).

Maximum Interest rates[j]	**Loans less than 7 years:** • $0 - $25,000: Base Rate[k] + 4.25% • $25,000 - $50,000: Base Rate + 3.25% • Over $50,000: Base Rate + 2.25% **Loans 7 years or longer:** • 0 - $25,000: Base Rate + 4.75% • $25,001 - $50,000: Base Rate + 3.75% • Over $50,000: Base Rate + 2.75%	**Loans $50,000 or less:** Cannot Exceed Prime[l] + 6.5% **Loans over $50,000:** Cannot Exceed Prime + 4.5%	Same as 7(a)[m]

Source: SBA.

[a]13 C.F.R. 120.120.

[b]13 C.F.R. 120.100.

[c]13 C.F.R. 120.101.

[d]13 C.F.R. 120.102.

[e]13 C.F.R. 120.110.

[f]Amounts listed are gross loan amounts.

[g]This fee cannot be passed to the borrower and SBA may charge the lender a late fee if the ongoing guarantee fee is not paid in a timely manner.

[h]This fee can be passed on to the borrower and is a one-time fee paid when the loan is approved or after initial disbursement.

[i]Packaging services" include the lender assisting the applicant with completing the application and preparing cash-flow projections and other documents related to the application. "Other services" include consulting as to what financing is needed and what type. The fees must be reasonable and customary for the services performed and must be consistent with those charged on the lender's similarly sized, non-SBA-guaranteed commercial loans. In addition, fees for packaging and other services may be based on a percentage of the loan amount.

[j]Lenders are permitted to add an additional 2 percentage points to the maximum interest rate listed for loans of $25,000 or less and an additional 1 percentage point to the maximum interest rate listed for loans between $25,000 and $50,000.

[k]For standard 7(a), there are three acceptable base rates: (1) the Prime Rate; (2) One Month London Interbank Offered Rate (LIBOR) plus 3 percentage points (LIBOR Base Rate); or (3) the SBA Optional Peg Rate.

[l]For SBA Express, a lender may use the same base rate of interest it uses on its similar non-SBA loans as long as the resulting interest rate does not exceed Prime + 6.5% or Prime + 4.5%, depending on the loan amount. However, if the loan is sold in the secondary market only the Prime Rate, LIBOR, and SBA Optional Peg Rate are permitted.

[m]Similar to SBA Express, a lender may use the same base rate of interest it uses on its similar non-SBA loans as long as the resulting interest rate does not exceed the amounts stated in the 7(a)'s maximum interest rates. However, if the loan is sold in the secondary market, only the Prime Rate, LIBOR, and SBA Optional Peg Rate are permitted.

Appendix III: GAO Contact and Staff Acknowledgments

GAO Contact	William B. Shear, (202) 512-8678 or shearw@gao.gov
Staff Acknowledgments	In addition to the contact named above, Andrew Pauline (Assistant Director), Benjamin Bolitzer, Daniel Kaneshiro, José R. Peña, Christine Ramos, Jessica Sandler, Jennifer Schwartz, Jena Sinkfield, and Andrew Stavisky made key contributions to this report.

www.ingramcontent.com/pod-product-compliance
Lightning Source LLC
Chambersburg PA
CBHW080851010626

R18375900001B/R183759PG45790CBX00007B/13